Using Technology

Other titles in the series Life—A How-to Guide

Choosing a Community Service Career
A How-to Guide
Library ed. 978-1-59845-147-4
Paperback 978-1-59845-312-6

Dealing With Stress
A How-to Guide
Library ed. 978-0-7660-3439-6
Paperback 978-1-59845-309-6

Friendship
A How-to Guide
Library ed. 978-0-7660-3442-6
Paperback 978-1-59845-315-7

Getting Ready to Drive
A How-to Guide
Library ed. 978-0-7660-3443-3
Paperback 978-1-59845-314-0

Volunteering
A How-to Guide
Library ed. 978-0-7660-3440-2
Paperback 978-1-59845-310-2

Getting the Hang of Fashion and Dress Codes
A How-to Guide
Library ed. 978-0-7660-3444-0
Paperback 978-1-59845-313-3

Using Technology

A How-to Guide

Life
A How-to Guide

Sherri Mabry Gordon

 Enslow Publishers, Inc.
40 Industrial Road
Box 398
Berkeley Heights, NJ 07922
USA

http://www.enslow.com

Library of Congress Cataloging-in-Publication Data
Gordon, Sherri Mabry.
  Using technology : a how-to guide / Sherri Mabry Gordon.
    p. cm.—(Life—a how-to guide)
  Includes bibliographical references and index.
  Summary: "Read about the different kinds of technology available today, including text messaging, the Internet, Facebook and MySpace, online games, and MP3 players. Also, find out how to stay safe in the digital world"—Provided by publisher.
  ISBN 978-0-7660-3441-9
  1. Information technology—Juvenile literature. 2. Cyberspace—Juvenile literature. 3. Internet and children—Juvenile literature. 4. Amusements—Technological innovations—Juvenile literature. 5. Digital electronics—Juvenile literature. I. Title.
  T58.5.G66 2011
  621.382—dc22
                    2010028430

Paperback ISBN 978-1-59845-311-9

Printed in the United States of America

082011 Lake Book Manufacturing, Inc., Melrose Park, IL

10 9 8 7 6 5 4 3 2 1

To Our Readers: We have done our best to make sure all Internet addresses in this book were active and appropriate when we went to press. However, the author and the publisher have no control over and assume no liability for the material available on those Internet sites or on other Web sites they may link to. Any comments or suggestions can be sent by e-mail to comments@enslow.com or to the address on the back cover.

Enslow Publishers, Inc., is committed to printing our books on recycled paper. The paper in every book contains 10% to 30% post-consumer waste (PCW). The cover board on the outside of each book contains 100% PCW. Our goal is to do our part to help young people and the environment too!

Illustration Credits: All clipart © 2011 Clipart.com, a division of Getty Images. All rights reserved.; © Andrea Gingerich/iStockphoto.com, p. 14; AP Images/Sean Kilpatrick, p. 107; © Chris Bernard/iStockphoto.com, p. 25; © Chris Schmidt/iStockphoto.com, pp. 69, 78; © Felix Möckel/iStockphoto.com, p.100; © FreezeFrame Studio/iStockphoto.com, p. 33; © Miodrag Gajic/iStockphoto.com, p. 46; © Nathan Gleave/iStockphoto.com, p. 76; © Rich Legg/iStockphoto.com, p. 80; Shutterstock.com, pp. 1, 3, 6, 9, 12, 20, 23, 28, 31, 36, 38, 44, 50, 53, 58, 62, 64, 66, 73, 83, 84, 85, 91, 92, 95, 101, 102, 105, 110, 111, 114, 128; © Willie B. Thomas/iStockphoto.com, p. 87.

Cover Illustration: Shutterstock.com (teen boy with laptop).

Contents

Wired!

Technology 4-1-1

T9, which stands for Text on 9 keys, is "predictive text" technology that can be used on cell phones. Other similar programs include iTap, eZiText and SureType. The goal of predictive text is to make it easier to type text messages. Once it is installed, words can be added to a text message by pressing a single key for each word. The result is easier and quicker texting.

Ultimately, quicker texting is accomplished by using a fast-access dictionary. As the technology becomes familiar with the words and phrases the user commonly types, it speeds up texting by offering the most frequently used words first. If the word it offers is not the one the user wants, he or she presses a predefined "next key" until the needed word is found.

Sixteen-year-old Ashley is a texting whiz. She does not even look at her cell phone while she taps out messages to her friends. With thirty to one hundred text messages coming in a day's time, it is a good thing.

Ashley says most of her texting consists of checking in with friends about everything from what happened in math class to plans for the weekend. Her mom, Janet, sets limits on the cell phone but says she likes the idea of being able to contact her daughters at a moment's notice.

Janet says:

> I really like that my kids are so accessible. For
> example, the other day the school had a bomb
> threat, and Ashley called me from her cell phone as
> she was leaving the building. So if she didn't have
> that cell phone with her, I would have been
> frantic. I know we survived at school
> without a cell phone all day long, but . . .
> kids today have so much more to deal
> with and all the crazy stuff that goes on
> in school.[1]

Like most teens her age, Ashley's cell phone is
not her only gadget. She also sports an MP3 player
from time to time and has her own laptop computer.
She is part of a growing segment of technologically
savvy teenagers who quickly recognize the benefits of new
technologies and are embracing them. In fact, 84 percent of
all teenagers own at least one personal media device such as
a laptop computer, cell phone, or personal digital assistant (PDA),
and 44 percent say they have two or more devices.[2]

Teens like Ashley realize that technology can help them
stay connected to others *between* face-to-face interactions, says
Scott Campbell, an assistant professor at the Department of
Communication Studies at the University of Michigan.

"Technology is not changing teens—they are in control,
they are taking advantage of the advances," he says.[3]

Just a Tap Away

Researchers believe tools like text messaging, instant messaging, e-mail, and social networking sites are popular among young people because being in close contact with their friends is important to teens like Ashley.

Perhaps Ashley's biggest passion is for her cell phone. A cell phone not only allows kids to stay connected, it also gives them the freedom they crave. No longer do they wait by the phone at home for a call from that special someone. Now they just give out their cell number and are on their way. In fact, many preteens cannot wait to get their own phones.

"It's a rite of passage," says Daniel Neal, cofounder of kajeet, the first pay-as-you-go cell phone service for tweens. "It's like the car keys when you were sixteen or seventeen. Now it's when you get your first phone."[4]

By far, the cell phone is a kid's favorite luxury. One survey found that many young people ages ten to seventeen would give up the radio, video games, MP3 players, and television before giving up their cell phones.

Kids are getting cell phones at younger and younger ages.

Cell Phone Etiquette

Directions: Test your knowledge of proper cell phone use. Discover how much you really know about proper phone etiquette.

1.) If you get a text message while in a restaurant or at a movie, what should you do?

    a) Wait until later. It is rude to read and reply to the message.
    b) Reply right away and then turn the phone off. It is rude not to respond immediately to the person sending the text message.
    c) Read the message, but respond later when there is a break.

2.) What should you do if you are expecting an urgent cell phone call from your parents, but you have a meeting scheduled with a teacher or a coach?

    a) Ignore the call and let voice mail pick it up.
    b) Warn your teacher or coach you are expecting an urgent call from your parents and may need to briefly leave the meeting to answer if it comes through.
    c) Put your phone on vibrate. If the call comes in, explain that it is your parents and leave to take the call.

3.) In which of the following places is it more acceptable to leave your cell phone on and take calls?

    a) In class at school
    b) At your friend's house
    c) While at the movies

4.) If you are visiting your girlfriend's/boyfriend's home for dinner, but are expecting a call regarding callbacks for a play you are auditioning for or a call from a college recruiter, how should you handle it?

    a) Tell the host (i.e., the parents) about the expected call. Then put the phone on vibrate.
    b) Keep the phone on and don't worry about it. Rules are relaxed in people's homes.

c) Put the phone on vibrate. If the call comes in, slip into the bathroom to take it.

5.) If you are having an important meeting (such as one with a college recruiter) or an important dinner (like an awards banquet) and your cell rings, what should you do?

a) Immediately turn off your phone.
b) Ignore the call and let voice mail pick it up.
c) Excuse yourself and take the call.

Answers: 1 – a, 2 – b, 3 – b, 4 – a, 5 – a

Tally up how many questions you answered correctly and then look below to see how you fared.

4–5 Correct = Ms./Mr. Manners

Congratulations! You are an etiquette expert. Most likely, you rarely offend people with your cell phone usage. Keep up the good work!

2–3 Correct = Borderline Bonnie/Bob

Your manners are borderline. Sometimes you know just what to do or say when it comes to your cell phone. Other times you struggle with common courtesy. Carefully consider your surroundings and you will soon become an etiquette expert.

0–1 Correct = Rude Rita/Randy

Your cell phone use is likely offensive to the people around you. Think twice before answering calls or replying to text messages. You need to make sure it is the appropriate time and place to use your cell phone.

Neal says part of the attraction is that cell phones help fill a need for connection, especially among kids with working moms or single parents. And if used properly, Neal says the cell phone can be a good communications tool. It helps families remain closer and involves parents in their kids' activities.[5]

Tapping Into Friendship

Perhaps one of the biggest appeals of the cell phone is its text messaging capabilities. Teens have found that texting is a fun and discreet way to talk with friends. Instead of passing a note in class, teens hide their cell phone in their lap and tap out a quick message (which, if caught, can get them in as much trouble). It also gives parents an easier way to touch base with their kids without an embarrassing conversation that friends can hear about who they are with and when they will be home.

"[Text messaging allows teens] to be connected but also disconnected at the same time because you don't actually have to talk to the person," says Dr. John Sargent, professor of

One reason teens like cell phones so much is their texting capability.

Technology 4-1-1

Text messaging (or texting) is also known as short message service (SMS). Text messages can be sent from a cell phone to another cell phone, an e-mail address, an instant messaging program, or a landline telephone. Typically, the message can be no longer than 160 characters in length.

psychiatry and pediatrics at Baylor College of Medicine and director of child and adolescent psychiatry at Ben Taub General Hospital. One positive, says Dr. Sargent, is that texting can help introverted teens make friends and feel more confident. However, teens can easily lose track of how many text messages they are sending and receiving.[6]

The World at Their Fingertips

Clearly, teens today are plugged into the world around them, and they are using the Internet to do it. In fact, nearly nine in ten teens are Internet users, according to the Pew Internet & American Life Project. Teens use the Internet for everything from e-mail, instant messaging, and social networking to online gaming and information gathering. Despite this trend, 13 percent of American teenagers do not use the Internet due to low income levels and limited access to technology.[7]

Teens use the Internet for many purposes—research, game playing, and communication.

Using Technology

How Teens Use the Internet

- 73 percent of teens use social networking sites

- 14 percent blog

- 8 percent use Twitter

- 38 percent share content

- 8 percent explore virtual worlds

- 62 percent read about current events

- 48 percent buy things

- 31 percent get health, diet, and exercise information

- 17 percent research sensitive health topics[8]

Let's B Friends

In addition to playing games and gathering information, teens also use the Internet to meet people—especially people with similar interests. Sure, they like hanging out with friends and talking. But the Internet gives today's teens more options. Unlike kids in their parents' day, they are not limited to fast-food joints, arcades, and skating rinks. If schedules and transportation make seeing each other in person an issue, they just connect online.

Are you tethered to your cell phone?

1.) When I am away from home my cell phone is:
   a) On me at all times, either in my pocket or clipped to my jeans
   b) Nearby in my purse, bag, or backpack
   c) On my dresser. I don't take it with me unless I really need it.

2.) The first thing I do in the morning is check my cell phone for messages and/or text my friends:
   a) Always—I do not start my day any other way.
   b) Probably the third or fourth thing I do after I brush my teeth and use the bathroom.
   c) I only check for messages in the morning if I have extra time or if I am bored.

3.) If my cell phone breaks or is damaged it would be:
   a) The end of life as I know it—my calendar and everyone's contact information is in my phone and I would be lost without it.
   b) Life would be a challenge until I picked out a new phone.
   c) No big deal. It was too bulky to carry around anyway.

4.) If I am going out with friends but then remembered that my cell phone was at home on the kitchen counter, I would:
   a) Freak out and demand the driver turn around so I can get my phone. I cannot go all night without a cell phone!
   b) Explain to the driver that I forgot my cell phone but leave it up to the driver about what to do. After all, I know how to use a pay phone.

16

Using Technology

c) Shrug it off. I don't need it anyway.

5.)   When I am out with friends and something funny happens, I:
  a) Reach for my cell phone, take a picture, and then send it
     to all my friends.
  b) Laugh along with my friends, but respect their privacy and leave
     my cell phone in my bag.
  c) Look confused … I don't see what's so funny.

To tally your quiz, give yourself five points for each "a," three points for each "b," and one point for each "c." Look below to see how you fared.

19–25 points = Tethered Tammy/Tommy
Your cell phone might as well be welded to your hip. It has become a part of your body and you cannot live without it! You probably never go anywhere without your cell phone, including the bathroom. In fact, a day without your phone might even cause withdrawal symptoms!

11–18 points = Manager Mindy/Mike
You use your cell phone quite a bit. But you are able to balance your cell phone usage with the rest of your life. You can see the convenience and usefulness of a cell phone but can just as easily manage life without it.

5–10 points = Carefree Claudia/Clarence
To you a cell phone is just another useless distraction in an already sensory-saturated world. You really do not see any value to cell phones. And you do not want to be so easily accessible to others. You prefer a little downtime every now and then and would rather not have the burden of lugging a phone around with you.

Their favorite hangouts? Facebook and MySpace. In fact, one study found that 86 percent of young people use social networking sites such as Facebook. For many teens it is simply an extension of the relationships they already have—another way for them to connect.[9]

In the beginning, MySpace was the king of social networking. For instance, in 2007, it was one of the most visited sites among U.S. Internet users and accounted for 4.92 percent of all Internet visits. At its peak in June 2007, the site had 7 percent of all Internet visits.[10] But Facebook has since closed the gap. In 2010, Facebook became the dominant social networking site in the United States with 500 million users.[11] MySpace is still one of the world's largest social networks with about 125 million users, but Facebook is more popular, especially among young people.[12] In fact, one report indicates that one-third of Facebook's registered accounts belong to people twenty-four years old and younger.[13]

Although MySpace and Facebook are similar in many ways, they were originally designed with different formats and purposes. For example, MySpace was created as a means for young people to interact with the culture around them by sharing music, videos, and more. On the other hand, Facebook was designed to connect college students to one another. Both sites have morphed to meet the needs of their users.

Using Technology

Yet despite their differences in popularity, both sites still have appeal. Research suggests that 20 percent of those visiting Facebook often visit MySpace right afterward. This pattern shows that even though the sites are different, many people choose to use both sites.[14]

Another popular social medium is Twitter. But surprisingly, teens do not use it as often as adults. While many of them have signed up for the service, they do not do much with it after that. Their reasoning? They do not want to waste credits on updating their Twitter accounts and would rather text their friends instead.[15]

It's All Fun and Games

Playing games online is very popular among young people. Part of the attraction is that going online to play games gives young people a lot more choices and some interesting opponents from all over the world.

Online game playing provides give-and-take as well as some interesting opponents.

Using Technology

Larry Magid, a technology columnist and commentator, claims that online gaming also offers some benefits. For instance, he says, players can learn how to compete and win, but they can also learn how to lose gracefully. Meanwhile, some games encourage cooperation and team building as well as bartering, negotiating, and other important social skills.[16]

However, there are some risks to online gaming, including the cost. Although some games are free, others have charges associated with them. Teens need to watch out for hidden or extra charges. They also need to be careful about giving out personal information. There is also the risk of being harassed by other gamers.

"If the conversation is making you uncomfortable, just end it," says Magid. "[And] if the game allows you to connect a webcam, be very careful about where you point the camera and what you are wearing."[17]

Talking 24/7

While e-mail is a popular way for teens to use the Internet, it is quickly losing its appeal. In fact, almost half, or 46 percent, say they prefer instant messaging [IM or IMing] to e-mail, according to a study for Pew Internet & American Life Project. The study also found that among middle-school and high-school kids "the popularity of e-mail and intensity of its use are waning in favor of IM."[18] With IM, teens can carry on several conversations at the same time.

Technology 4-1-1

IM users can have one or more real-time conversations at the same time. These conversations take place in windows that pop up on a user's computer screen. Teens that use instant messaging a lot often use "buddy lists." Buddy lists contain the screen names of conversation partners that users have entered into their accounts. The lists show which users are online and logged into the instant messaging program at any given time.

But Naomi Baron, a linguistics professor at American University, says she worries that it is more of a distraction than an accomplishment. "If you have fifteen conversations going simultaneously," she says, "sometimes you are just throwing things out there and then dashing off to the next customer."[19]

According to an AP-AOL survey:

- Almost half of teens, 48 percent of those thirteen to eighteen, use instant messaging (more than twice the percentage of adults who use it).

  Almost three-fourths of teens send instant messages more than e-mail.

- More than half of the teens who use instant messages send more than twenty-five a day and one in five sends more than one hundred.

- Teen users are almost twice as likely as adults to say they can't imagine life without instant messaging.

  Teens are more likely to use instant messaging to keep in contact with a friend who is far away, while adults are more likely to use e-mail.

- About a fifth of teens who use instant messaging have used it to ask for or to accept a date.

- About 16 percent have used instant messaging to break up with someone.[20]

IMing lets teens talk to friends in real time, no matter where they are.

Then and Now

Directions: Match the item or activity of your parents' generation (under "Then" column) with the item or activity of your generation (under "Now" column).

Then

1.) Portable cassette player

2.) Private telephone line (vs. party line)

3.) VCR (to record movies)

4.) Typewriter

5.) Passing notes

6.) "Mix" tapes

7.) Autograph book

Now

a.) Facebook

b.) Laptop

c.) Cell phone

d.) MP3 player

e.) TiVo

f.) Texting

g.) Download music

Answers:
1 – d, 2 – c, 3 – e, 4 – b, 5 – f, 6 – g, 7 – a

Using Technology

In addition to writing to each other, teens also use instant messaging to share links, photos, music, and videos.

Music to Their Ears

Finally, today's teens are always on the go, and devices that are portable are attractive. With the creation of MP3 players, teens can now take their music with them too. Nearly four in five teens, or 79 percent, have an iPod or an MP3 player.[21] Most teens use their MP3 players to listen to music, but they can also be used to listen to audiobooks, and many can also be used to watch videos.

MP3 players have become increasingly popular. In fact, 85 percent of 12- to 24-year-olds prefer the iPod to the radio.

Technology 4-1-1

MP3, which stands for MPEG Audio Layer 3, is the most popular form of compressed digital audio file. MP3 allows users to download audio files such as music and books. These files can be transferred to a portable listening device called an MP3 player.

One study found that teens prefer MP3 players to the radio as the way to get their fill of music, with 84 percent of fourteen- to seventeen-year-olds listening to music daily on MP3 players and only 78 percent listening to the radio daily.[22] With MP3 players and music-playing features on smartphones, teens can control what they want to hear and when they want to hear it. Such instant gratification is not as easily attained by listening to the radio, where the audience is often at the mercy of short playlists and busy request lines. It is no surprise then that devices that make people and information more accessible and portable will be the hot items among today's teens.

The Family
Interface

Technology has become so integrated into the life of today's teenager that it is changing the way the American family interfaces (or communicates). In fact, for today's teen, it is often hard to tell where the online life ends and the offline life begins. Large chunks of time are consumed with texting, instant messaging, checking Facebook accounts, and surfing the Internet. Meanwhile, many parents are struggling just to keep up. As a result, experts are asking how technology impacts daily family life.

Among today's teens, it can be hard to tell where the online life ends and the offline life begins.

Part of technology's draw is that teens are going through the growing-up process, including separating from their parents, and technology helps them to do that. "Unfortunately though, in many homes the use of all media technologies has resulted in more isolation," says Nancy Willard, director of the Center for Safe and Responsible Internet Use. "In the evening, it is every kid on his or her own computer—or watching TV or a video in his or her room. So parents need to work overtime to ensure that family members also do things together as a family."[1]

On the plus side, if parents learn to use technology effectively, teens will remain more involved with their families. In fact, nearly one in three teens, or 29 percent, who use IMs or text messages use them to communicate with parents.[2]

"Instead of the once-a-week telephone call from a parent to a child in college, they can communicate and remain involved more regularly," Willard adds. "I expect to be able to have greater ongoing communications and connections with my kids when they leave home for college because of these connecting technologies."[3]

Willard is the author of the books *Cyberbullying and Cyberthreats* and *Cyber-Safe Kids, Cyber-Savvy Teens.* She has three children, ages sixteen, fourteen, and ten, and understands the frustrations and challenges today's parents face. How many family dinners grow cold or are rushed through because the kids can't peel themselves away from the computer? But she emphasizes how important it is to help kids find a balance between spending time with 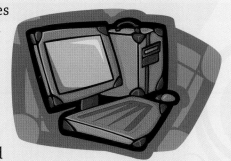 media and participating in real-life activities, such as playing sports, hanging out with friends, doing homework, and completing chores. She also discusses the appropriate behavior she expects from her kids and the possible online risks they may face.

And her time has been well spent. Willard recalls her fourteen-year-old daughter showing her a message she had received from a guy. "He [saw] her pictures and [said] she was very 'hot.' My eyebrows went up—but my daughter quickly told me 'Don't worry, mom, I have already blocked him.'"[4]

Natives and Immigrants: The Technology Gap Between Parents and Teens

Some parents are out of touch with the technologies that have captivated their teens. They lag behind their kids and sometimes allow their inexperience to turn into skepticism. Meanwhile, other parents are trying to keep up with emerging technologies but are recognizing that they just are not as savvy as their kids.

According to Willard, "There is definitely a gap. This gap is similar to the gap felt by immigrant parents with children born in the new culture. What we have to recognize and come to accept is that [as parents] we 'digital immigrants' will never, ever feel as comfortable with these new technologies as [our children] the 'digital natives' do."[5]

What happens, explains Willard, is that when a person's brain develops, it does so in a manner that fits with the culture he or she is growing up in. For instance, the brains of children who grow up speaking Chinese function differently from the brains of children who grow up speaking English. As a result, a teen who is immersed in a technologically saturated culture will be wired differently from his or her parents, who did not grow up with as many gadgets.

Many adults may not fully understand the online world, but they have better decision-making skills and are much less susceptible to manipulation and peer pressure. These are lessons kids can't acquire through any Web site. They need to be learned from their parents.

Breaking the Code

Kids today want to communicate—but on their terms, says Dr. Ruth Peters, a clinical psychologist, author, and parenting expert. She says kids and parents can use cell phone options

Because today's young people have grown up with technology from a very young age, they are more comfortable with it than their parents.

and text messaging to connect in meaningful ways. She offers the following examples of how cell phones can benefit the parent-child relationship:

- Parents can get quick answers to their questions when they text their children. Such questions might include "What time is practice over?" and "When will you be home?"

- Texting takes "tone of voice" out of the mix, so teens and parents are less likely to get defensive with one another.

- Texting allows parents to enter their child's world and communicate in a style they are used to.

- Texting vs. calling gives kids the space they crave while allowing parents to keep in touch as often as necessary.

- Texting can strengthen the parent-child bond and let kids know their parents are thinking of them. For instance, parents can send an encouraging message before soccer tryouts or a big test.

- Parents can also use the camera and video functions of cell phones creatively. For example, if an older teen is seeing a concert with friends, parents can ask them to shoot some video to share with them at home. Likewise, parents who travel for work can send photos to their kids.[6]

Learning the Lingo

As texting and instant messaging become increasingly popular among teens and many adults, a new language is emerging. Users have come up with a type of shorthand that allows them to say more in one message. For example, people do not use punctuation, and they often remove the vowels from words.

As text messaging has become more popular, a new language has emerged that allows people to communicate in a type of shorthand with fewer characters.

Decoding the Lingo

Here's a chance to quiz your parents and determine just how much they really know about texting lingo. Make a copy of this quiz and see if they can "decode" the text messages below.

Lingo	Decoded Message	Lingo	Decoded Message
1.) BTW	_____	14.) U	_____
2.) TTYL	_____	15.) NE1	_____
3.) LOL	_____	16.) RYT	_____
4.) POS	_____	17.) PPL	_____
5.) Y?	_____	18.) LUV	_____
6.) PLZ	_____	19.) HF	_____
7.) CUL8R	_____	20.) GUDLUK	_____
8.) TY	_____	21.) PTB	_____
9.) BCUZ	_____	22.) EM?	_____
10.) LMIRL	_____	23.) CYR MA	_____
11.) IMO	_____	24.) CYR PA	_____
12.) IMNSHO	_____	25.) KIT	_____
13.) 4	_____		

Answers: 1.) By the way 2.) Talk to you later 3.) Laugh out loud 4.) Parent over shoulder 5.) Why? 6.) Please 7.) See you later 8.) Thank you 9.) Because 10.) Let's meet in real life 11.) In my opinion 12.) In my not so humble opinion 13.) For 14.) You 15.) Anyone 16.) Right 17.) People 18.) Love 19.) Have fun 20.) Good luck 21.) Please text back 22.) Excuse me? 23.) Call your mother 24.) Call your father 25.) Keep in touch.

After tallying how many your parents deciphered correctly, determine which category they fall into: 18–25 Correct = Texting Titan   9–17 Correct = Somewhat Savvy
0–8 Correct = Techno Phobe

Words like "text" and "message" become TXT and MSG. Users also replace words with symbols and numbers. Instead of typing "to" or "for," they will use "2" and "4." Finally, users use sounds and abbreviations to represent words.

Balancing Act

If your parents are concerned about your use of technology, they are not alone. Experts say that parents need to take an active role in ensuring that their kids are able to balance their use of technology with everyday life—especially when it comes to spending face-to-face time with others. The goal is to show kids that it is valuable to slow down and unplug for a while.

At Janet's house, she and her daughters spend several Friday or Saturday nights each month "without gadgets." Instead of texting and checking Facebook, they spend time as a family having dinner or just hanging out. Her daughter Ashley has come to appreciate the need to slow down. In fact, Janet says Ashley has set some personal limits on her use of technology. Instead, she is trying to carve out time to pursue some of her other interests, including painting and exercise.

David Levy, a professor at the University of Washington Information School, has found that many of his students are concerned about the obsession with multitasking. In fact, in an informal poll he found that students were concerned about how plugged in they were and "the way it takes them away from other activities including exercise, meals and sleep."

Some teens become so engrossed by their gadgets, the rest of the world seems to disappear. They don't even take the time to properly greet their family members.

Using Technology

"Although it wasn't a scientific survey," he says, "it was the first evidence I had that people in this age group are [asking] these questions."[7]

Family Dynamics

Janet says she sees how technology and multitasking can steal time and become an obsession for her kids. So she tries to limit her kids' inclination to multitask, especially if they are doing homework. They focus solely on their assignments. Only once the homework is done can they text, IM, or go onto Facebook. She hopes that her limits will help her kids learn to prioritize and manage their use of technology rather than letting technology consume them.

"I'm not certain how the children can monitor all those things at the same time, but I think it is pretty consequential for the structure of the family relationship," says Elinor Ochs, director of UCLA's Center on Everyday Lives of Families and the leader of a four-year study of modern family life. "[One thing we have observed] is that when the working parent comes through the door, the other spouse and the kids are so absorbed by what they're doing that they don't give the arriving parent the time of day."[8] The kids were too busy with their gadgets to manage anything more than a mechanical "hi," if they greeted the returning parent at all.

"The problem," concludes Edward Hallowell, psychiatrist and author of *CrazyBusy*, "is what you are not doing if the electronic moment grows too large . . . you are not having family dinner, you are not having conversations, you are not debating whether to go out with a boy who wants to have sex on the first date, you are not going on a family ski trip or taking time just to veg. It's not so much that the video game is going to rot your brain, it's what you are *not* doing that's going to rot your life."[9]

Multitasking—by doing homework, surfing the Web, and listening to music all at the same time—is not the most efficient or healthiest way to work.

Using Technology

Computer Time Log

Directions: Make a copy of the Computer Time Log and keep it next to your computer. Each time you get on the computer, fill in the amount of time you spent online and what you were doing. If you get on the computer multiple times in a day, put a plus (+) sign between each set of minutes and total the time at the end. At the end of the week, look at how much time you spent IMing, e-mailing, surfing, and playing games. If you are having trouble getting your chores done or your homework completed, you may want to think about where you can spend less time online. You also want to be sure you allow time for eating healthfully, exercising, and getting enough sleep.

Monday

I spent _____ minutes IMing my friends.

I spent _____ minutes checking and writing e-mail messages.

I spent _____ minutes on a social networking site (such as MySpace or Facebook).

I spent _____ minutes playing games or in a virtual world.

I spent _____ minutes surfing the Internet for personal enjoyment.

I spent _____ minutes using the computer to work on homework.

Tuesday

I spent _____ minutes IMing my friends.

I spent _____ minutes checking and writing e-mail messages.

I spent _____ minutes on a social networking site (such as MySpace or Facebook).

I spent _____ minutes playing games or in a virtual world.

I spent _____ minutes surfing the Internet for personal enjoyment.

I spent _____ minutes using the computer to work on homework.

Wednesday

I spent _____ minutes IMing my friends.

I spent _____ minutes checking and writing e-mail messages.

I spent _____ minutes on a social networking site (such as MySpace or Facebook).

I spent _____ minutes playing games or in a virtual world.

I spent _____ minutes surfing the Internet for personal enjoyment.

I spent _____ minutes using the computer to work on homework.

Thursday

I spent _____ minutes IMing my friends.

I spent _____ minutes checking and writing e-mail messages.

I spent _____ minutes on a social networking site (such as MySpace or Facebook).

I spent _____ minutes playing games or in a virtual world.

I spent _____ minutes surfing the Internet for personal enjoyment.

I spent _____ minutes using the computer to work on homework.

Friday

I spent _____ minutes IMing my friends.

I spent _____ minutes checking and writing e-mail messages.

I spent _____ minutes on a social networking site (such as MySpace or Facebook).

I spent _____ minutes playing games or in a virtual world.

I spent _____ minutes surfing the Internet for personal enjoyment.

I spent _____ minutes using the computer to work on homework.

Saturday

I spent _____ minutes IMing my friends.

I spent _____ minutes checking and writing e-mail messages.

I spent _____ minutes on a social networking site (such as MySpace or Facebook).

I spent _____ minutes playing games or in a virtual world.

I spent _____ minutes surfing the Internet for personal enjoyment.

I spent _____ minutes using the computer to work on homework.

Sunday

I spent _____ minutes IMing my friends.

I spent _____ minutes checking and writing e-mail messages.

I spent _____ minutes on a social networking site (such as MySpace or Facebook).

I spent _____ minutes playing games or in a virtual world.

I spent _____ minutes surfing the Internet for personal enjoyment.

I spent _____ minutes using the computer to work on homework.

Week Totals

Total hours spent IMing my friends _____

Total hours spent checking and responding to e-mails _____

Total hours spent on a social networking site _____

Total hours spent playing online games or in a virtual world _____

Total hours spent surfing the Internet for personal enjoyment _____

Total hours spent using the computer to work on homework _____

Conclusions: Now that you have calculated your computer time, what did you discover?
If you want to try to balance your computer time with time spent doing other things, where can you cut back? _____

_____

Overall, the way teenagers and parents deal with the constant rush of technology in their lives will influence the adults these young people become. Sure teens can teach adults a lot about how technology can be utilized. But parents have something to offer too. They need to be sure their kids have a life beyond the screen.

Big Brother Is Watching

Some companies are cashing in on the paranoia technology has created in parents. For instance, some companies are equipping cell phones with GPS (global positioning systems). This service allows parents to locate their kid's phone within a few blocks.

But some experts believe parents should focus on communicating more and monitoring less. Without communication, "technology gets in the way of just having a decent social relationship," says Robbie Blinkoff, a consumer anthropologist who has studied cell phone usage among parents and teens. He says parents and teens should negotiate how they will use cell phones—on both sides.

Although the cell phone can appear like a tool for rebellion with kids using it to keep adults in the dark, the cell phone also can help kids bond with their parents, he says. "It often tethers the relationship."[10]

Another tool for parents to monitor their kids' activities is a two-way video link, which can be done via Wi-Fi on the iPhone 4 and iPod Touch. "Then it won't just be 'Where are you?' but

Experts say it's important for teens and parents to communicate about Internet use.

'Show me what friends are at the party,'" says Jeffrey Belk of Qualcomm, who has three daughters of his own. "That would be really mortifying."[11]

Parents Who Get It

According to Anastasia Goodstein, the author of *Totally Wired*, despite the paranoids, there are parents who get it. They understand that technology is here to stay and that the answer does not lie in "turning it off," nor does it lie in letting kids do whatever they want. These parents realize that their teens know more about how to use technology or certain Web sites. But this does not keep them from engaging with their kids.

"They ask their teens to show them what they are doing, what sites they visit and how they work," she says. "In the process, they open up a dialogue where they [can reinforce] their values about how to be online, how to treat people online ethically, and what it means to have a public site."[12]

She says parents can also teach their kids how to be media literate and critical of what they see, as well as address issues such as online pornography. Instead of distancing parents and kids, technology has the potential of bringing them closer together.

Totally Connected!

Sometimes being on the Internet is so much fun that you don't realize how much time has passed.

It is Sunday afternoon, and thirteen-year-old Claire is grounded until Tuesday. She spent five hours on MySpace when her daily limit is two hours. Like most teens, she lost track of time—a common pitfall with today's technology.

This is not uncommon, says Nancy Willard. "Most teens today are in constant communication with each other.

I recently took my children on a business trip with me. Despite being far away from her friends, my fourteen-year-old daughter was in almost constant contact with her friends back home—through her cell phone and social networking site. She and her friends were texting each other throughout the day—when her friends were in school."[1]

For teens with healthy peer relationships, this additional means of connection appears to be enhancing and deepening relationships, says Willard. But the technology is also helping troubled teens connect with others like them, perhaps reinforcing negative attitudes and behavior.

Willard also indicates that teens often spend as much time using different forms of media as they do sleeping. Some kids even sacrifice several hours of much-needed sleep to their gadgets.

R U Awake?

For instance, Claire is supposed to be in bed by 8:30 P.M. each night. But she likes to stay up texting her friends. One night she sent out a mass text message without thinking. Her mom, Janet, recalls:

> She forgot that her mother and her sister are on her text message list. So it is 9:37 P.M. and I get a text from her with a little poem that said . . . "Thank you for making me laugh more and cry less." . . . I'm looking at it and I can't believe she is

up there pretending to be asleep but is really texting her friends. So I sent her a text back saying: "You just made me laugh less and you are about to cry more." . . . Needless to say though, no more phone in her room at night.[2]

Everyone knows that teens are often sleep deprived. But technology could be making the problem worse. And the biggest culprit is text messaging. Much like surfing the Internet or watching television, texting energizes teens rather than helps them fall asleep. As a result, text messaging is a major contributor to sleep deprivation, says Dr. Cora Breuner, a pediatrician at Children's Hospital and Medical Center and mother of a teenage son. "Every ping of an incoming message is a temptation to pick up the phone. They know talking on the phone might wake up their parents, but if they text, it probably won't."[3]

The ABZs of Sleep

Research has shown that teenagers need more sleep than adults. In fact, they need, on average, nine hours of sleep per night. But the American Academy of Sleep Medicine found that 30 percent of U.S. teens do not get enough sleep. As a result, these sleep-deprived kids could be putting themselves at risk.[4]

For example, sleep deprivation weakens the immune system. This leaves a person more susceptible to diseases and disorders such as diabetes, cancer, and even the common cold.

Lack of sufficient sleep also increases stress, which in turn can upset a person's mental processes. The consequences may result in confusion, memory loss, irritability, and even emotional highs and lows. Moreover, sleepy people find it hard to focus on what they are doing, so schoolwork can suffer and driving may be impacted. For instance, drowsiness and falling asleep at the wheel cause more than 100,000 car crashes every year.[5]

Other consequences of sleep loss include:

- forgetting important information like names, numbers, homework, or a date with that special someone

- acne and other skin problems

- yelling or other inappropriate behavior

- overeating, especially unhealthy foods such as sweets and fried foods, which can lead to weight gain[6]

Getting an adequate amount of sleep each night is important. When you get a good night's sleep, you wake up feeling refreshed and alert. Sleep also affects how we look, feel, and act. If you are getting enough sleep, you will feel better overall. But if sleep is cut short, the body doesn't have time

Some teens find that their use of cell phones and other gadgets gets in the way of a full night's sleep.

to complete important functions such as regulate growth and appetite, make repairs, and improve your mind. This loss then shows up in weight gain, sickness, and difficulties with mood and memory. Here are some tips for getting more sleep:

- Figure out when you have to get up. Then count backward eight and a half to nine and a half hours to find out when you should be asleep. Give yourself an extra half hour to get ready for bed.

- Make a weekly schedule and plan each day's activities. Make the rest of your activities fit in around your sleep schedule.

Getting Your ZZZs

Directions: Answer yes or no to each of the following questions.

1.) Do you struggle to get out of bed for school?

      a)   Yes   b)   No

2.) Do you have trouble staying awake in class?

      a)   Yes   b)   No

3.) Do you sleep until noon on the weekends and/or take naps on the weekends?

      a)   Yes   b)   No

4.) Are you grouchy and/or moody with your friends and family?

      a)   Yes   b)   No

5.) Do you often forget things?

      a)   Yes   b)   No

6.) Do you get about six and one half hours of sleep per night or less?

      a)   Yes   b)   No

7.) Do you feel sleep is overrated?

      a)   Yes   b)   No

If you answered "Yes" more times than "No," then you likely are suffering from what is known as sleep debt. What this means is if you do not get enough sleep during the week, your body will try to make you "pay back" the sleep that you owe, just like when you borrow money from someone. Sleep debt causes your body to sleep longer on weekends, fall asleep in class, or struggle to get out of bed.

- Avoid exercising, eating, and consuming caffeine two hours before bed.

- Get relaxed before bed by dimming the lights, listening to relaxing music, or reading.

- Use your bed for sleeping and not for other, more stressful activities, such as homework.

- Turn off your computer and your cell phone. To resist the temptation of using your phone, leave it charging in another room.[7]

Keep in Touch

According to Willard, technology helps teens continue valuable friendships beyond geographical boundaries. It also keeps them more involved with their families.

"When I grew up, if a friend moved away, [we would try to stay connected by writing letters]," she says. "In most instances this became infrequent communication and the friendship dissolved." But technology does pose some risks and teens must come to realize that. For instance, "life" can be much more public.[8]

Teens are at the point in their lives where they are trying to figure out who they are. They might explore different personal identities, and much of their self-expression is now done online. Unfortunately, teens often post the bad along

Many parents monitor their kids' computer use, especially among younger teens.

How Big Is Your Safety Net?

1.) When someone asks to be my "friend" on MySpace or Facebook, I:

    a) Look at his or her picture and profile and if he or she looks cool, I say yes. The more friends the better, right?

    b) Am cautious about who I have as "friends." I know people are not always who they say they are and I am careful about adding strangers to my friends list. Besides, I don't see MySpace or Facebook as a popularity contest.

2.) People who visit my page on my favorite social networking site are most likely to see photos of:

    a) Me in a bathing suit . . . My friends and I doing crazy things . . . In fact, the crazier, the better. I want people to know that I like to have F-U-N.

    b) A few photos of me with my friends and/or my pets. I would never post photos that I would be too embarrassed to show my parents, my school's principal, or a college recruiter.

3.) When it comes to my personal information and my MySpace/Facebook page, I:

    a) Include as much information about myself as I can. I want people to know who I am, where I live, and what I am all about.

    b) I never give out information that would make it easy for a stranger to find me, including my phone number, my address, my IM screen names, my passwords, or even where I hang out every day after school.

Using Technology

4.) If someone writes a rude, crude, or hateful comment about me on my MySpace/Facebook page, I:

    a) Reply with something just as offensive. I can flame others just as well as the next person. No one says something mean to me and gets away with it.

    b) Tell my parents or another trusted adult. I know they will be able to help me handle the situation by reporting it to the proper authorities and blocking the person's access to my page.

5.) If someone begins to threaten me or make sexual comments to me through my MySpace/Facebook page, I:

    a) Ignore it or make fun of them, hoping they will go away.

    b) Tell my parents or another trusted adult. I know sexual harassment and threats to harm me physically are against the law.

6.) If someone I meet online asks me to meet them in person, I:

    a) Agree to a date and time. I love to meet new people.

    b) Tell my parents or another trusted adult that my new friend wants to me meet me. I know it is not smart to agree to meet people alone when I have never met them.

Tally how many "a's" you have and how many "b's" you have. Give yourself one point for every "a" and three points for every "b." Now see how you did:

16-18 points – Great job! You are a safe socializer.

12-15 points – Safety alert! You may need to increase your security.

6-11 points – Security breech! You are taking risks online and need to beef up your security soon!

with the good. Inappropriate photographs or comments can affect reputations, personal relationships, and job opportunities down the road. Teens need to be cautious about the kinds of stuff they are allowing others to see online.

Younger children need even more assistance staying safe. For instance, adults need to limit children's access to only preapproved sites and modes of communication, or "safe places."[9]

Three basic rules for children include:

1.) Don't go outside of the safe places without an adult.

2.) Never type your name, address, or phone number online.

3.) If something "yucky" comes on the screen, turn it off and tell an adult.[10]

When kids start communicating with others online, they also need to know that if someone sends them a hurtful or inappropriate message they should leave the situation, block the sender if possible, or file a complaint. If they are not sure what to do or if what they do does not work, they should ask for assistance from an adult.

Another challenge, Willard adds, is the fact that teens are meeting other people online. While it is true that the majority of the people teens meet have a connection with someone they know in person and are perfectly safe, there are some who could be dangerous. Teens have to learn how to evaluate the safety of an online aquaintance and recognize when others are trying to manipulate them.

Creative Texting

Young people are getting creative when it comes to technology use—especially text messaging. In fact, they are finding it can be used for a variety of situations. For instance, twenty-one-year-old Holly used texting to get out of a scary situation one night while visiting a nightclub. When six guys surrounded her and her friends on the dance floor with requests to leave for some after-hours fun, she used texting to get help.

"[When the guys would not take no for answer], I sent a message to my guy friend telling him to come get me," Holly says. "And about five minutes later, he was there to grab us from the crowd."[11]

John Johnson, a spokesperson for Verizon Wireless, says the growth of text messaging can be traced back to the September 11 tragedy. People in crisis realized that their text messages got through when cell phone voice lines were jammed, he says. Likewise, parents and kids used texting to communicate during the Virginia Tech shooting. And colleges are looking into ways to use texting to reach their students during emergencies.[12]

Local school districts also use mass texting to notify parents and students when school is canceled or delayed due to bad weather. Even nightclubs are tapping into the texting craze. Using the Web site clubtexting.com, management lets their patrons know about upcoming entertainment. An assistant at one nightclub says he can reach one thousand patrons at once.

Totally Connected!

Many teens say they have begun relationships through texting or e-mail—and a number have broken up remotely as well.

Using Technology

"You don't have to worry about doing it yourself, texting one by one, thousands of people," says Ti' Jean Beezer, an assistant in the Love nightclub, located near Washington, D.C. "It's very effective."[13]

The Instant Message Shield

Kids often use communication tools like e-mail, texting, and instant messaging to say things to each other that they would never say in person. For instance, they might not be able to find the words to break up with a boyfriend or girlfriend, so they will send a message instead. Or, they might be really angry at a close friend and shoot them an angry message. Teens are finding that technology can function as a shield during uncomfortable situations.

They hide behind it to avoid something potentially embarrassing or to say things they would never have the courage to say face-to-face. In fact, about half of girls and more than a third of boys say they have used IM to say things they would not say in person. For instance, nineteen-year-old Lewis says he uses instant messages to ask for dates and to break up. Fear of rejection prompts him to ask for dates through IM, in which case he can just close out the window if things don't go smoothly. Lewis says there are advantages to the IM breakup too.

"I've had some crazy ex-girlfriends. Saying that in person would probably not be the best idea for my physical safety," he says.[14]

Technology 4-1-1

Experts at Web Wise Kids ask visitors to their site: "So you have your own blog, your own e-mail account, maybe even your own computer. [But] when it comes to life and the Internet, do you think you know it all? . . . You might not. For instance, do you know what a friend is? Friends are people we know in real life, not people we only know online. You don't tell personal things to people on the street. So don't tell personal things to just anyone online."[15] The site also warns kids against making friends with strangers online. Some adults trying to make friends with kids may be up to no good or may even be criminals.

Setting the Tone

Over the years, teens have become adept at managing the technology in their lives—especially their cell phone calls. Obvious tools include caller ID and voice mail, but ring tones are really catching on. For instance, teens often assign their best pals specific ring tones so they know who is calling. This allows them to let some calls go unanswered while others get answered immediately.

Young people are also downloading high-frequency ring tones. They have found this is a way to receive text messages without being detected by adults—specifically, teachers and other school officials. Many teachers cannot hear the ring because of what is known as aging ear. What this means is that as people mature, they lose the ability to hear high-frequency sounds.

High-frequency ring tones were not developed with this purpose in mind. In fact, they are a spin-off of technology meant to bother teenagers, not help them. A Welsh security company developed the tone, called "Mosquito," to help store owners. The owners would play the tones in front of their stores to discourage teens from hanging out there. Meanwhile, the adult customers were not affected.[16]

Not surprisingly, ring tones have become a growing business, especially among teens. However, the high-pitched tones are not the only tones selling. Some ring tones are even making it into mainstream music. In 2005, a ring tone was incorporated into a song called "Crazy Frog," which beat out a new release by Coldplay on the British pop charts. And Billboard.com launched a Top 40 Ring Tone Chart in October 2004. The first number-one tone to hit the chart was "My Boo" by Usher and Alicia Keys. It sold 95,000 copies.[17]

Technology 4-1-1

A recent survey by the American Speech-Language-Hearing Association found that more than half of high-school students had lost some hearing because of MP3 players. Their symptoms included the need to turn up the volume of the TV, saying "What?" or "Huh?" in a normal conversation, and experiencing ringing in their ears. This is known as noise-induced hearing loss and comes from listening to MP3 players, or other electronic gadgets with earphones, for too long and with the volume too high. Because the condition is permanent, experts recommend that teens turn down the volume, limit their listening time, and switch from earbuds to sound-isolating earphones or headphones.[18]

Loud MP3 players can damage hearing permanently. Experts recommend sound-isolating earphones rather than earbuds.

Using Technology

There are many reasons why kids fall in love with ring tones. They help them evade the rules in school and they help them manage their incoming calls. But perhaps the biggest attraction is that ring tones allow teens to express themselves. By listening to people's ring tones, you can tell what kind of music they like and even what kind of sense of humor they have.

Chapter 4

Rebooting School

School administrators and teachers are always looking for ways to deal with the intrusion of new technology into the classroom.

Connecting with others using technology has become a way of life for teens. In fact, it is deeply embedded into their lifestyle. But when a technologically reliant teen walks into school, it can be hard to adapt to a new set of rules—especially rules that limit technology. Most schools find that cell phones and iPods interfere with classroom instruction. These devices can also be used to cheat on exams and to invade others' privacy.

Yet some teens are not deterred by school rules. They have become very adept at texting on the sly and are finding ways around school rules. In fact, some are so skilled at texting that they can tap out a message without ever taking the cell phone out of their pocket. It is second nature to them.

For instance, schools officials at Westerville City Schools in central Ohio say it is not unlikely for teens to try to sneak in a text or two during the school hours, especially during lunchtime or during study hall. But the use of cell phones is strictly prohibited during school hours.[1]

Teachers and administrators across the nation worry that all the technology is causing students to become disconnected from the people around them. Instead of greeting people as they walk to class or socializing with their friends during lunch, students have their ears plugged into their iPods and their eyes glued to their phone screens.

When Wired Kids Come to School

It is no big secret that today's young people are wired. For instance, Diane Conley, senior executive director of curriculum and instruction in Westerville City Schools in Ohio, estimates

Even when they're hanging out, many kids still pay more attention to their gadgets than their friends.

Using Technology

that 85 percent of the district's students have Internet access. What's more, some kindergarteners have cell phones, more than 50 percent of middle-school students have them, and nearly all high-school students have cell phones.[2]

Still, schools are faced with the challenge of reaching and teaching technologically savvy students. Conley says one way that her district is addressing the changing needs of today's students is through a new curriculum.

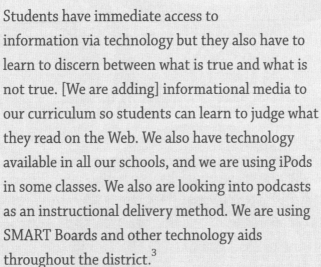

> The world is an open book to students. Research is both easier and more difficult. Students have immediate access to information via technology but they also have to learn to discern between what is true and what is not true. [We are adding] informational media to our curriculum so students can learn to judge what they read on the Web. We also have technology available in all our schools, and we are using iPods in some classes. We also are looking into podcasts as an instructional delivery method. We are using SMART Boards and other technology aids throughout the district.[3]

Yet some educators worry about the potential of excluding those students who do not have access to technology. While research demonstrates that technology can have a positive impact on student learning, it will have a limited impact on achieving district-wide goals if not all students can participate. There are still students without access to the Internet. Typically, they come from poorer backgrounds, and a large number are minorities. But when schools—especially those with students from disadvantaged homes—focus on practical uses of the Web, they can increase the opportunities for at-risk youth by giving them marketable skills.[4]

Is the System Crashing or Rebooting?

Twenty years ago the student-to-computer ratio was one computer for every 125 students in school. Today there is one computer for every 3.8 American teens. What's more, 99 percent of schools have Internet access. And many have digital whiteboards instead of chalkboards. Yet many teens feel their school is lagging behind when it comes to technology. In fact, when asked to grade their school's technology, teens gave their teachers and the school's extracurricular activities higher marks than their school's technology.

One possible explanation for the schools' low grades could be that many districts across the country are facing tightening budgets. These issues delay system upgrades and postpone the replacement of older computers. And as computers get older and the money for maintaining them is scarce, some classes may find themselves without computers at all. This could prove to be particularly frustrating for teens with high expectations of available technology.[5]

Not all schools measure up to the high-tech needs of today's students. Tight budgets can mean there is not enough money to keep computers and software current.

What's the Write Way?

Because technologies such as instant messaging and text messaging are so new, educators are just starting to recognize the effects they may have on students. It's no secret that constant communication impacts a student socially. But how does the incessant IMing and texting impact kids academically? This is what teachers across the nation want to know.

Pass or Fail? Grade Your School's Technology

Directions: Read each question below and decide whether you would give your school a passing grade or a failing grade. Then, brainstorm ideas on how you can help your school improve its available technology.

1.) My school has enough computers in each classroom.   Pass or Fail?
2.) My teachers incorporate technology into the classroom. Pass or Fail?
3.) My school makes good use of technology. For instance, I can e-mail and/or text my teachers with questions about schoolwork. Pass or Fail?
4.) My teachers maintain class Web sites with information that is useful. Pass or Fail?
5.) My school's technology policies are appropriate, easy to follow, and enforced fairly.   Pass or Fail?

Overall Grade_____ [Your school passes if they received more passes than fails. Your school fails if they received more fails than passes.]

My ideas on how to improve my school's use and availability of technology:

_____

_____

My ideas on how I can encourage my school to consider improving its availability of technology: _____

_____

Basically, there are two opinions regarding the effects of instant messaging on students. The first is that the new lingo used during IM and texting, sometimes called "Internet English," is a breakdown of the English language. Meanwhile, others see Internet English as an example of how language is constantly changing. They also see it as a type of literacy that can be used to engage students in more traditional learning.

According to Amanda O'Connor, a graduate student studying digital literacies, students who frequently communicate through IM do not even realize they are including IM lingo into their academic writing because they are so used to it. As a result, their assignments are fraught with bad grammar and punctuation and abbreviations that do not belong in formal writing. On the other hand, says O'Connor, some teachers think it's great that kids are so comfortable expressing themselves through writing, even if it is by IMing.[6]

Adapting to the IM Trend

Some teachers are realizing that a teen's interest in IMing and texting can be used to help students do well in school. For example, Trisha Fogarty, a sixth-grade teacher, says that she does not mind how her students spell things during the first draft of their papers "as long as they are writing."

"If this lingo gets their thoughts and ideas onto paper quicker, the more power to them," she says. However, she does expect that when they revise their papers, they correct their usage of the English language.[7]

And Robyn Jackson, a high-school English teacher, has organized an online chat room where students meet once a week to discuss literature and writing. "The students are allowed to use Internet-speak in the chat room that would never be allowed in formal writing, but the online conversations are vigorous and intelligent."[8]

Jackson then uses the chat room as a tool to teach students when it is appropriate to use their informal language and when it is not. It is not something that comes automatically to them. She believes this is a rule students need to be taught.

Robert Schrag, a communications professor, agrees. "We have always . . . taught our children different language structures and how they function in different arenas," he says. "We use [a different] language structure watching a basketball game than in our place of worship. Most children will understand the difference."[9]

Drawing the Line

When it comes to online teen activity, schools and law enforcement are attempting to help draw the line. For instance, many schools are beginning to hold students responsible for what they post online. In Libertyville, Illinois,

Online discussions on topics studied in class are one way some teachers are using technology to help students learn.

the school board unanimously voted that students in extracurricular activities sign a pledge. The pledge states that evidence of illegal and inappropriate behavior could be grounds for discipline.[10]

Meanwhile, a group of teenagers from two different high schools was arrested in Lombard, Illinois, for underage drinking. Officials say they learned about it through Facebook. In fact, four students shown drinking were charged with possession of alcohol and the hostess of the party was charged with contributing to the delinquency of a minor. Overall, nineteen students were identified from the photos and eleven of them were student-athletes. As a result, they were suspended from 20 percent of their sports seasons.[11]

Cracking Down

Many teens cannot leave home without their cell phone clipped to their belt and the earbuds to their iPod wedged in their ears—especially when going to school. Many schools have rules regulating the use of these devices during class hours. Yet kids across the country break these rules every day. As a result, schools are cracking down and handing out tougher penalties.

For instance, any student caught using a cell phone at Ashley's school, Pickerington Central High School in Ohio, will lose the phone until the end of the day. If it happens again, then parents have to pick up the cell phone at school. If a student is caught a third time, he or she cannot have the cell phone back until the end of the school year.

The Hillsborough school district in Florida has proposed the following rules for using electronic devices such as cell phones and MP3 players during school hours:

- First offense: a warning and the device is taken away.

  Second offense: the device is confiscated until the end of the day and the school notifies the parent.

- Third offense: the device is taken away, parents are notified, and the student receives detention.

- Fourth offense: the device is taken away, parents meet with administrators, and the student gets an in-school suspension for one to three days.

  Future offenses: the student may receive an out-of-school suspension.[12]

Many teachers welcome the policies because cell phone usage distracts students from learning. Others are most concerned about kids downloading inappropriate material, such as pornography, onto their iPods and bringing it to school.

In many schools, students caught using a cell phone will have the device confiscated.

Using Technology

Modern-Day Cheat Sheets

When it comes to cheating on tests, some students always seem to find a way. From writing the test answers on their hands to scribbling notes on the brims of their hats, a few kids have always tried to beat the system. But today's technology seems to be making it a little easier.

Only recently have teachers realized that cell phones are sometimes used for cheating. Students can text the answers to their friends or store the answers inside their phones. Then they discreetly access them during the test. So when schools started banning cell phone usage, teens seemed to be one step ahead. The latest trend is to use MP3 players, such as iPods, to cheat. The tiny devices can easily be hidden under clothing with the wire to the earbud snaked behind an ear and tucked into a shirt collar. Meanwhile, formulas and other material have been downloaded onto the player.[13]

The Web of Deceit

One in every five American teenagers admits to using the Internet to plagiarize material for school assignments, according to a poll conducted by CBS News in 2006. Kathleen Frankovic, the director of surveys, says the actual number may be higher because people have a hard time admitting they have done something wrong. Overall the survey found that 24 percent of the boys and 14 percent of the girls said that they had used the Web to cheat at least once.[14]

Students go over a research project with their teacher. In 2006, 20 percent of American students said they had used material from the Internet without proper credit.

If You Can't Beat 'em, Join 'em

Some teachers believe the best approach is to find ways for tech-savvy students to use their devices in schools. For instance, Jerry Foust, a music teacher, has incorporated iPods into the curriculum. He has his sixth graders develop podcasts on African music and culture.

"Almost all of my students have iPods, so I try to come up with stuff that's more relevant to them and interesting. We're going to upload stuff of interest, so that people around the world who are doing research on this topic will come across our kids' podcasts," Foust says.[15]

Duke University began providing iPods to its students several years ago. It was part of an experiment to see how the devices could impact learning. As a result, MP3 players have proved to be extremely useful in some courses, specifically music, engineering, and sociology, says Tim Dodd, executive director of the Center for Academic Integrity at Duke.

"Trying to fight technology without a dialogue on values and expectations is a losing battle," says Dodd. "I think there's kind of a back-door benefit here. As teachers are thinking about how technology has corrupted, they're also thinking about ways it can be used productively."[16]

Exploring Technology's Risks

Texting and driving—even if you can text with just one hand—can be a deadly combination.

Although it is not a regular occurrence, twenty-year-old Sarah says she knows how to text her friends while driving. "I don't even have to look at my phone," she explains, "I can tap out a message [with one hand] and still keep my eyes on the road."

Yet, Sarah says she refrains from texting unless it is really important. "Even though I could do it if I wanted, I know it's not very safe to text my friends and drive at the same time especially in heavy traffic or pouring rain," she says.[1]

Still, Sarah is the exception to the rule. In fact, many young people often do not realize how dangerous texting and driving at the same time can be—especially for inexperienced drivers. In fact, a recent insurance survey found that despite the risks, more than one-third of all young drivers send text messages while driving and that one-fifth of all drivers text while behind the wheel.[2]

YouTube has videos of young people texting and driving, and in 2008 about six hundred Facebook members joined a group called *I Text Message People While Driving and I Haven't Crashed Yet!* The group was started by twenty-one-year-old Taylor Leming from Virginia as a joke among friends. However, she acknowledges that texting while driving is dangerous and if her state made it against the law, she would follow it.[3]

To date, Taylor has had some close calls but has never been in an accident. But not everyone is as fortunate. There have been numerous traffic accidents caused by young drivers talking on the phone or sending and receiving text messages.

For example, an eighteen-year-old Arizona girl was distracted while she was texting, which caused her pickup truck to cross a lane and smash into another car. The forty-year-old driver of the other vehicle was killed in the crash. And a June 2007 head-on collision in New York that killed five teenagers also may have been connected to text messaging. The kids, who had all graduated from high school just five days earlier, were riding in an SUV that swerved into oncoming traffic, hit a tractor-trailer, and burst into flames. Just moments earlier the seventeen-year-old driver of the SUV had sent and received text messages.[4]

"When cell phones first came out, I thought they were the greatest productivity tool ever created," says David Teater, a Michigan man whose twelve-year-old son was killed in a traffic accident in January 2004. The driver of the other vehicle said she was distracted by a cell phone conversation that caused her to drive her Hummer through a red light and slam into the car the boy was riding in. "After that accident, I looked at the research and was shocked to find out how dangerous it is to conduct a telephone conversation while driving," Teater says.[5]

Today, he works for a company that is researching ways to make cell phones safer and easier to use, especially while driving. For instance, the company is experimenting with technology that would sense when a phone is in driving mode and keep the driver from being distracted while driving.

Let's Talk Safety

Distracted driving—whether it is from a cell phone call, a text message, a new CD, or a hamburger—is a major cause of car crashes each year. In fact, the American Automobile Association says that between four thousand and eight thousand of the

Taking your eyes off the road for just a few seconds to text can result in a serious accident.

crashes that happen each day in the United States are due to distractions such as cell phones. In a year, these distractions account for as many as 3 million of the 6 million car crashes.[6]

As a result, many states are developing laws that make it illegal for people to use a cell phone or other electronic devices while driving. Details of the laws vary from state to state. Some have laws that apply just to teens; others apply to all drivers. Some permit hands-free calling; some do not.

When Virginia was considering its ban on cell phone use, House of Delegates member Timothy Hugo illustrated the danger by sending a text message to the House floor. Hugo said that in the seven seconds it took him to punch in the message, a car driving 60 miles per hour could cover the length of two football fields—200 yards of road the driver isn't watching.[7]

Against the law or not, using a cell phone while driving puts you at a higher risk of getting into a crash!

In September 2007, California joined a number of other states and D.C. in banning teen cell phone use when driving. When making their decision, California lawmakers received a report from the California Highway Patrol that said driver cell phone use is a primary cause of accidents. It was accompanied by a Ford Motor Company study that found teens are four times more likely to be distracted than adults by cell phone use.[8]

"While we are driving, we are bombarded with visual information. We might also be talking to passengers or talking on the phone," says Rene' Marois, PhD from Vanderbilt University. "Our research [shows] . . . that the brain cannot . . . do two things at once. People think if they are using a headset with their cell phone while driving they are safe, but they're not because they are still doing two . . . demanding tasks at once."[9]

You may wonder how talking on a cell phone is any different from talking to someone in the car. The difference is that you may take your hands off the wheel to answer or make a call, which makes it easier to lose control of the car.

Hold the Phone!

When it comes to driving, cell phones, and text messaging, teens should keep these points in mind:

- Recognize that driving requires a person's full attention.

- Use cell phones only when your car is in park.

- Ask a passenger in the car to make a call for you and speak in your place.

The safe way to text in your car is to pull over and park first.

Exploring Technology's Risks

Safety Patrol: What's Your Cell Phone Safety IQ?

1.) How much does your collision risk increase when you use a cell phone while driving?
   a) 100 percent   b) 400 percent   c) 50 percent

2.) What percent of cell phone–related crashes are due to incoming calls?
   a) 33 percent   b) 25 percent   c) 42 percent

3.) Which state was the first one to make it illegal to use a cell phone while driving?
   a) New York   b) Texas   c) California

4.) The best way to substantially reduce the risk involved with cell phone use while driving is to:
   a) Use a hands-free device
   b) Use the speaker phone on your cell phone
   c) None of the above

5.) Talking on a cell phone while driving can be as dangerous as:
   a) driving and eating
   b) driving drunk
   c) driving with a car full of people

Answers: 1 – b, 2 – c, 3 – a, 4 – c, 5 – b

- Inform the person you are calling that you are speaking from the car and tell them you will call back later.

- Secure your phone in the car so it does not become a projectile in a crash.[10]

- Check out the laws in your state regarding cell phone use.

Using Technology

Playing Games

Everyone enjoys a good game now and then. It is natural to want to compete with another person—to test your skills and see how you fare. But online games can become a problem when kids use them to escape—or worse yet, when they become a compulsion. It is then that they become an addiction. In fact, addiction to computer and online games is a real and growing problem, with nearly one in ten kids between eight and eighteen addicted to online gaming.

One report on gaming addiction says, "The most addictive games are the online multiplayer games. They include role-playing, endless levels of achievement, and an IM or chat function. Groups of players play and chat online, creating a fantasy world that provides an escape from real life. Kids can get caught up in this fantasy world to the exclusion of their real-life responsibilities."[11]

Interest in video and computer games can reach the level of an addiction.

As a result, some kids spend hours on the computer and let everything else slide. They lose interest in school, forget to turn in homework, then their grades drop. They stop hanging out with their real friends and would rather be at home playing games with "online friends." They also become obsessed. All they can talk about are the games they are playing and how well they are playing them. And when people challenge them about how much time they spend playing games, they try to hide their behavior. Finally, gaming addiction takes its toll in sleeplessness, dry eyes, and even repetitive-stress disorders, such as carpal tunnel injury, which causes weakness, numbness, or pain in the hands.

There are also other risks to obsessive gaming. For instance, it can be expensive and dangerous. Aside from lots of money for extras, the chat feature of games can expose kids to online predators.

But keep in mind that spending a lot of time playing games is not the same as an addiction. When you are addicted to something, it takes over your life. It damages personal relationships and takes a toll on your physical and emotional health.

Most kids who play online games are just having fun and are not doing themselves or anyone else any harm. Everyone is entitled to a brief escape from reality every now and then. But if you think that you or someone you know has an addiction to computer games, it is best to talk with a trusted adult—a parent, a teacher, or a school psychologist. A gaming addiction is very much like an addiction to drugs or alcohol. Sometimes it requires professional help.

False Courage

Every day we hear stories about teenagers who do and say things in the cyberworld that they would never say or do in real life—especially face-to-face with a real person. The cyberworld allows them to loosen up. They relax and let down their guard. And they express themselves without really thinking about the consequences. In fact, this happens so often that researchers have developed a name for it. It is called online disinhibition effect.

Basically there are two types of online disinhibition: *benign* (harmless) disinhibition and *toxic* (harmful) disinhibition. With benign disinhibition, people might share personal things about themselves such as their secrets, fears, dreams, and goals. They might be somewhat different from the way they are in real life—for instance, sillier or more outgoing. Toxic disinhibition, on the other hand, is characterized by rude language, critical remarks, anger, hatred, and even threats. "It also involves visiting the underworld of the Internet—places of pornography, crime, and violence—territory they would never explore in the real world," says John Suler, PhD, from the department of psychology at Rider University.[12]

With benign disinhibition, Dr. Suler says that people are attempting to better understand themselves, resolve interpersonal problems, or explore their identity, which is sometimes called "working through" things. On the other hand, toxic disinhibition is "acting out . . . without any personal growth at all," he says.[13]

Basically, there are a number of factors that contribute to the online disinhibition effect in people. At the top of the list is the idea that their words and actions feel anonymous and that they cannot see other people so they feel invisible.

Feeling invisible also gives people the courage to do and say things they would never dream of doing and saying face-to-face. Communicating electronically saves them from having to deal with people's physical and verbal responses. But seeing a frown on someone's face or hearing a sigh can cause people to think twice about what they are saying or are about to say. Not having face-to-face cues can result in misinterpretations because the reader of the message has to assume the tone of voice and look on another's face. The absence of real time also means a teen can say something and then not have to cope with the person's response for minutes, hours, days, or sometimes even months.[14]

Finally, online interactions minimize the status or authority of a person. In real life, people are often shy about saying what they really think in front of an authority figure. They might be concerned about disapproval or even discipline. Yet the Internet provides everyone with an equal opportunity to voice his or her opinions.

"[P]eople are much more willing to speak out and misbehave," Suler says. "The traditional Internet philosophy [says] that everyone is equal, that the purpose of the net is to share ideas and resources among peers. . . . This [idea] contributes to the minimizing of authority."[15]

In the end, kids may inadvertently find themselves in trouble with authority figures if they are not careful.

Many teens express themselves via the Internet in a positive way. But some teens use it to lash out at others and spread hostility.

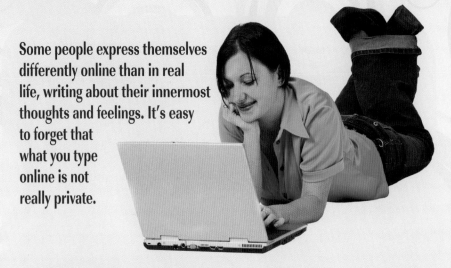

Some people express themselves differently online than in real life, writing about their innermost thoughts and feelings. It's easy to forget that what you type online is not really private.

Too Much Information

Kids used to write their thoughts and feelings in diaries that they kept under lock and key. Now technology has encouraged teens to disclose more. But they may not understand the consequences of such behavior.

"Teens don't think of posting something online as public acts, so they are horrified when their dad reads it," says Lee Rainie, Pew Internet & American Life Project. "Posting on MySpace . . . feels like a solitary act even if the outcome could be seen by millions. Even in e-mails, we often write things we would not dare to say aloud to another person."[16]

Technology can also allow teens to get "validation for any bizarre or antisocial attitude of belief they have," says Dr. James Garbarino, a chair in humanistic psychology at Loyola University. For instance, Garbarino says that after the Columbine school shooting in 1999, kids developed a site called "The Church of Dylan and Eric," which was seeking approval for the boys' actions. Garbarino believes that online activity encourages depersonalization. The Internet offers kids anonymity, which makes it easier for them to post terrible things online without fear of being punished.[17]

Sometimes, though, teens do not mean for their private thoughts to become public, but they later find that an e-mail they sent to one person was later forwarded to a hundred people at school, and now everyone knows what they think of the math teacher, how they feel about elevators, or who they have a crush on. As technology becomes more and more a part of our lives, young people need to grow more cautious about what they say to one another. Here are some other tips for maintaining privacy:

- Don't send personal information, such as your social security number, passwords, or PIN numbers to anyone. That information can be stored in their cell phone, in their e-mail account, or on their computer.

- Put a password on your cell phone, on your IM account, and on your e-mail. This will prevent others from accessing your private information or pretending to be you.

- Erase all your personal information before selling, recycling, or donating your cell phone. Sometimes this can be done using a "master reset" feature.

- Remember that no matter how secure you have made things, the ultimate security of your private messages depends on the person receiving them.[18]

Too Many Things at Once

Scientists are discovering that multitasking, or dividing one's attention into small pieces and parts, impacts the way young people learn, reason, socialize, do creative work, and understand the world. On one hand, this learned skill helps prepare kids for today's busy workforce. But experts believe that multitasking may also impact the quality of a person's work. Furthermore, experts are concerned that kids do not have enough downtime to relax and reflect.

An article in *Time* magazine pointed out the social and psychological impacts of multitasking: "If you are IMing four friends, watching *That 70s Show*, it is not the same as sitting on the couch with your buddies or your sisters and watching the show together or sharing a family meal across the table.

Technology 4-1-1

Experts at Web Wise Kids ask: "Do you know that a picture is worth a thousand words? What do the pictures you post online say about you? A sexually explicit or suggestive photo tells the world how you feel about yourself. Photographs are like advertisements. Are you valuable and interesting, or are you cheap and sleazy? Sleazy pictures attract sleazy people. Or, do you know how dumb—and dangerous—it is to communicate online with people who say sexual things to you? How gross is that? They don't have a life and they think you don't have one either. Prove them wrong. Tell them to get lost. Get offline and go hang out with your real friends."[19]

Using Technology

If you're with a group of friends, taking time out to text and answer your phone means you are not as engaged in the social situation.

. . . The facial expressions, body language [that are missed] puts broadband to shame in its ability to convey meaning and create bonds."[20]

What's more, the ability to do many things at once has its limits. Trying to do two or more things at once increases errors. And it takes longer to do the work—double the time or more, says David E. Meyer, director of the Brain, Cognition and Action Laboratory at the University of Michigan. "The toll in terms of slowdown is extremely large—amazingly so," he says. "If a teenager is trying to have a conversation on a chat line while doing algebra, she'll suffer a decrease in efficiency, compared to if she just thought about algebra until she was done.

Internet Safety Contract

Directions: *Make a copy of this Internet Safety Contract and review it with your parents. Space is provided below for you and your parents to add more guidelines. After you all have agreed to the guidelines, sign and date the contract and post it near your computer as a reminder of what you have agreed to do.*

- I will follow my family's guidelines for being online, including when I can be online and for how long.

- I will follow my family's guidelines for what sites and chat rooms I can and cannot visit.

- I will keep my personal information private. This includes my full name, my address, my cell phone number, my home phone number, and my school name and address.

- I will send appropriate pictures of me, my family, and my friends only when I have permission from my parents.

- I will be kind and respectful to others at all times while I am online. This includes not making hurtful or threatening remarks or comebacks.

- I will be honest and truthful about who I am. This includes not using someone else's screen name, pretending to be someone I am not, or lying about my age. If for safety reasons, I need to change any information, I will discuss it with my parents first.

Using Technology

- I will discuss all privacy settings with my parents and honor their wishes on how much information is shared and with whom.

- I will tell my parents or another trusted adult immediately when someone sends me a harassing or threatening message.

- I will tell my parents or another trusted adult when someone I met online asks me to meet him or her in person.

- I understand that not everyone I meet online is who they claim to be and I will be careful about whom I invite to be my "friends."

- _____

   _____

- _____

   _____

- _____

   _____

My Signature_____ Date _____

Parent's Signature _____ Date _____

People may think otherwise, but it's a myth. With such complicated tasks [you] will never, ever be able to overcome the . . . limitations in the brain for processing information during multitasking. It just can't be."[21]

The brain needs rest and recovery time to consolidate thoughts and memories. So teenagers who fill every quiet moment with a cell phone call or some other type of communication may not be getting the break they need. Instead, they may lose their ability to concentrate all together.

Policing the Social Sites

The headlines are filled with the stories of worst-case scenarios of what can happen on social networking sites. From the sixteen-year-old girl who flew as far as Jordan to marry a West Bank man she met on MySpace to the foureen-year-old girl who killed herself after a local mother posing as a boy bullied her, these stories are raising red flags among parents, elected officials, and law enforcement.

Predators are particularly attracted to social networking sites because of the ease with which they can get personal information. For instance, in chat rooms predators have to have a conversation with a person to get to know him or her. But on sites like MySpace, they have access to loads of information just by reading a user's profile, comments from friends, and blog entries, and looking at photos.

Unfortunately, many kids receive unwanted sexual solicitation over the Internet. But they are getting smart. In fact, a survey by the Pew Internet & American Life Project found that two-thirds of teenagers keep their profiles private and nearly half include false information.

"A lot of teens have been bombarded by the message that social networks are not safe. This is something teens are living with and swimming with every day and that's reflected in the steps they're taking," says Amanda Lenhart, a senior research specialist with Pew Internet and coauthor of the survey.[22]

But there are still too many teens including personal information, such as full names and cell numbers, in their profiles and putting themselves at risk.

Technology and Drugs

Experts are finding that some American teens are using text messaging and the Internet to keep up their drug habit. In fact, one teen receiving drug treatment at the Pathway Family Center in Indianapolis says he used the Internet to look for new ways to get high. And when his parents wanted to do a drug test, he went online to find out how to detox so his test would be clean. He says he also linked his instant messenger to his favorite drug sites so that his friends could find them too. Another patient says her cell phone was her most important tool for drugs. She kept her dealers' numbers in her phone under other names so nobody would find out.[23]

Exploring Technology's Risks

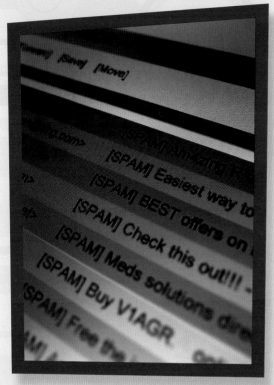

SPAM e-mails offering deals on drugs are constantly sent to people's inboxes.

But teens do not have to be looking for drug information to be at risk, says John P. Walters, Director of National Drug Control Policy. Bogus pharmacies flood e-mail inboxes with prescription drug offers and "drug dealers lurk in chat rooms just like pedophiles, targeting teens with offers of drugs."[24]

Furthermore, one study found that the Internet leads adolescent drug users to try new drugs and drug combinations; take steps to minimize the harmful effects of drugs; and modify the use of preferred drugs.[25]

Not So Bad?

But is all this technology really that bad? Some experts believe the benefits far outweigh the risks. Brendesha Tynes, a professor of educational psychology and African American studies at the University of Illinois, believes that when teens

The Internet is a great research tool and medium for self-expression, but you should always think about what you're saying and whom you're talking to.

engage in online discussions, they have an opportunity to develop critical thinking and reasoning skills. They also can "find support from online peer groups, explore questions of identity, get help with homework, and ask questions about sensitive issues they might be afraid to ask face to face," she says. They can also improve their ability to understand another person's point of view.[26]

Tynes believes the key to keeping teens safe online is not restricting the technology, but instead talking to them about it. Adults can help teens stay safe by working with them to "develop an exit strategy," she says. "Teens should know how to warn or block persons who make them feel threatened and how to [remove] themselves from uncomfortable situations."[27]

Chapter 6
Technology Revolution

This generation of teens is the first to be completely at ease using technology such as cell phones to keep in touch with their families and friends.

This generation of teenagers is the first to grow up digital. They are becoming adults in a world where computers, the Internet, online games, MP3 players, and cell phones are common. And they are the first generation where it is the norm to express themselves. Technology also has made them used to rapid change and given them unique skills. As a result, they will challenge companies in the future, says Dr. Patrick Dixon, chairman of Global Change and Europe's leading futurist:

> Today's teens often do many things at once: simultaneously watching YouTube, doing homework and talking on [their cell phone are a breeze]. They prefer Internet chat to e-mail, which is slow and boring. They are seasoned Internet researchers and they share themselves, their thoughts, hopes and creative products with the world. To older generations, this behavior seems unfocused, even dangerous, but by 2012, when these kids are graduating, it will be an asset.[1]

Social Networks Becoming Mobile

One trend teens are experiencing is social networking sites on cell phones. MySpace and Facebook have developed applications that allow customers to fully access the sites on their mobile phones.

Much like social networking online, mobile social networking happens in virtual communities. In most mobile communities, cell phone users can create their own profiles, make friends, create and participate in chat rooms, hold private conversations, share photos and videos, and share blogs by phone. What's more, mobile communities are becoming more and more popular among young people.

For instance, Rave Wireless has created a number of cell phone applications that connect college students to their campuses, their teachers, their fellow students, and even campus security through social networking on cell phones. In 2006, fifteen colleges and universities in the United States were offering their students a way to know what was happening across campus in real time. From finding out about canceled classes and updated homework assignments to pinpointing a friend's location on campus, students know what's happening— and not happening—where and when. The folks behind Rave say it makes the transition from high school to college easier and reinforces a sense of community among students.[2]

Tapping Into the Texting Trend

As texting becomes more and more a way of life for teens, adults are exploring ways in which they can use texting to reach young people—especially when the messages may involve life and death. For example, doctors in Cincinnati are experimenting with text messages that remind teens to take their medications. Many young people with chronic conditions, such as asthma and diabetes, do a poor job caring for themselves. But now doctors are trying to determine if texting reminders may help them take their meds on time.

According to experts, the teen years are an awkward time. Not only are their parents turning over more

Using Technology

Text reminders can help kids remember to take their medications.

Technology Revolution

responsibility, but it is also a time when teens do not want to be different. This is particularly true if it means taking regular medications and eating special diets. In fact, some studies suggest that only half of kids properly follow treatment steps.

So when Dr. Maria Britto, an asthma specialist at Cincinnati Children's Hospital, noticed that the kids on her exam tables often kept texting even while she was talking to them, an idea was born. She realized that kids as young as twelve from all income brackets carry cell phones into her clinic. As a result, a text reminder might help them manage their illness.

The study's goal is to determine if texting a daily reminder would improve kids' asthma control. Participants tell the clinic what time they want a reminder. Then a clinic volunteer types out the messages. Researchers are hoping it will help prevent attacks, improve school attendance, and decrease doctor's visits. If the simple reminders work for asthma, they may work for other diseases too.[3]

Cornering the Teen Market

Most teens do not realize that sites are capturing their personal information to be used for advertising, says Nancy Willard. But many companies are looking into ways to target trendsetting teens. For instance, teens really like those cute personality quizzes, she says. "They do not [realize] these are market research [tools] . . . that when they provide their contact information, which is necessary to see the results of the quiz, that they are giving permission for the company to sell their information to anyone. When they see the term 'privacy policy' they think that this means the site has a policy of keeping their information private. They have not read the fine print in which the company states that they will use and sell their information to anyone."[4]

MySpace and other networking sites are tightening their security to protect their young members, but teenagers still should understand how companies gather their personal information to market to them.

Cell Phone Solicitation

One way advertisers are getting their messages to teens is through the cell phone. According to a study of junior-high and high-school students, 17 percent of teens reported receiving

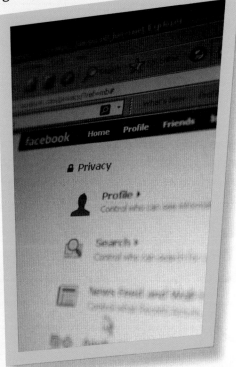

A Facebook page. Many users do not understand the degree to which social networking sites will use their personal information.

advertisements on their cell phones. The study also found that 48 percent of teens surveyed send text messages from their cell phones.

Michael Hanley, an advertising professor at Ball State University, predicts advertising will increase as more and more marketers get cell phone numbers. "With 24 million teens having cell phones, it's no wonder advertisers want to tap into this market," he says. "As cell phones become multimedia communications devices, we'll see advertisers start to send three- to five-second commercials and more interactive messages. Although it seems like a short period of time as compared to 30-second television commercials, it's long enough to get a brand across and show a product."[5]

iPod Therapy

As technology infiltrates our society, more and more people are finding creative uses for electronic devices. Aside from being used in schools, other professionals are finding creative ways to utilize iPods. For instance, a University of Mississippi researcher used iPod Shuffles to help people who stutter. His patients used the iPods to hear speech and imitate the sounds at the same time. His initial findings showed that people did speak more naturally. Doctors also are making use of the iPod. In another study, people training to be physicians listened to recorded heartbeats. As a result, they were better at recognizing abnormal patterns with their stethoscopes.[6]

Libraries Embracing Technology

Teens are often reluctant to approach a librarian for help. So public libraries across the country are starting to embrace the idea of using instant messaging in their reference areas as a way to interact with teens. For instance, Carnegie Library in Pittsburgh, Pennsylvania, launched an IM pilot program in its teen reference section in 2005. What they found is that instant messaging:

- fosters a relationship between teens and librarians

- creates intrigue for teen patrons

- provides critical information in a convenient and immediate way

- provides a "permanent" format for teens if they choose to save the interactions

The library also benefited from instant messaging because it allowed them to document the interactions and study them at a later date. Instant messaging also provided a way for the librarians to communicate library policies to teens in an informal and friendlier way. The only downside was that teens sometimes abused the service. For instance, teens might request bogus titles or become rude if they did not receive an immediate response. But overall the library found IMing with its teen patrons helped them to become more inviting.[7]

Librarians are finding that some teens are more comfortable
communicating with them through IMs rather than face-to-face.

Using Technology

Technology and Teens in the Future

Willard predicts that all technology in the future will be mobile and interactive. "Young people, especially teens, will have devices in their back pocket that provide complete Internet access—anywhere, anytime," she says. "This includes in the classroom—where they will demand to be able to use their own personal device to conduct research, engage in note-taking, and work collaboratively with their peers."[8]

For instance, Willard says, when the Internet came into schools it was generally perceived as an extension of the information resources—similar in nature to the research resources in the library. But teens today need more than just a digital library; they need interaction. Schools and businesses need to adapt to the new technologies to stay relevant with teens.

The future of Internet use will likely involve smaller and smaller devices.

Technology 4-1-1

The MIT Media Lab wants to see every young person with a laptop—especially those in struggling countries. The new XO Laptop is a stripped-down machine with a sun-friendly screen that is perfect for kids in developing countries. The folks behind the XO hope that by giving each child his or her own laptop, they will be able to bridge the gap in learning that has existed for years between developing countries and countries like the United States. The $150 price tag is designed to encourage governments to buy them in bulk.[9]

All in all today's teens were born into a connected world. They want to be recognized for their blogs, gaming avatars, online friends, and photos. To them, this is an extension of who they are. And all this connectivity helps them join dozens of different groups.

Today's teens will also be the first group to have a full digital history online. Everything they ever posted will be floating around in cyberspace—good things, and unfortunately the bad things as well. The challenge, then, that faces today's teen is to learn how to harness the freedom and portability that today's technology offers and express themselves in ways that will not haunt them later in life.[10]

Cyberbullying

Some teens may experience cyberbullying while online. Cyber-bullying occurs when one young person is targeted by another young person using the Internet, mobile phones, and other technologies. When an adult is involved, that is called cyber-harassment or cyberstalking.

About one-third of all teenagers who use the Internet say they have been targeted by a cyberbully, including receiving threatening messages, having online rumors spread, and embarrassing pictures posted. But of all the types of online harassment, most teens have had their private communications forwarded or publicly posted without their permission.

There are a number of ways to prevent cyberbullying, including never posting or sharing personal information online, such as your address, telephone number, passwords, school name, credit card number, or social security number. You also should never agree to meet publicly with someone you have never met.

Additionally, you should carefully consider everything you post online. In other words, ask yourself, could this message or photo be taken out of context? What would my teachers or my parents think if they read or saw this online?

Even if you are careful, you could still become a target. If you are being harassed online, it is best to leave the area (i.e., chat room, online gaming area, instant messaging). If you are being harassed through e-mail or instant messaging, block the person sending the messages and never reply.

Unfortunately, cyberbulling can be very harmful, causing teens to feel angry, hurt, embarrassed, or scared. In extreme cases, it has been linked to school violence, suicides, fights, and physical harm among teens. If you are cyberbullied or harassed, save all communication with the cyberbully and talk to a parent, teacher, law enforcement officer, or another trusted adult. Report the harassment to your Internet Service Provider. If the bully is making physical threats, report those threats to the police.

Chapter Notes

Chapter 1. Wired!

1. Author's interview with Janet Young, March 2008.

2. Amanda Lenhart, Mary Madden, and Paul Hitlin, "Teens and Technology: Youth Are Leading the Transition to a Fully Wired and Mobile Nation," *Pew Internet & American Life Project,* June 27, 2005, <http://www.pewinternet.org> (October 20, 2007).

3. Daniel Schorn, "Cell Phones: Evolution or Revolution?" *CBS News,* June 13, 2006, <http://www.cbsnews.com/stories/2006/06/08/gentech/main1695676.shtml> (January 29, 2008).

4. Tiffany Capuano, "The 411 on Cell Phones: A Parent's Guide to Understanding the Cell Phone Boom Among Kids," *Atlanta Parent Online,* n.d., <http://www.atlantaparent.com/07-09-September2007/sept07-art3-cell-phones.html> (March 25, 2011).

5. Ibid.

6. Baylor College of Medicine, "Teens Tap Into Text Messaging Craze," *eMaxHealth,* May 15, 2006, <http://www.emaxhealth.com/cms//?m=show&opt=printable&id=5894> (January 29, 2008).

7. Lenhart, Madden, and Hitlin.

8. Kristen Purcell, "Teens, the Internet, and Communication Technology," *Pew Internet & American Life Project,* June 25, 2010, <http://www.pewinternet.org/~/media/Files/Presentations/2010/Jun/Purcell%20YALSA%20PDF.PDF> (March 25, 2011).

9. Derek E. Baird, "Study: Facebook and MySpace Enhance the Positive Relationships Kids Already Have," *Barking Robot,* January 27, 2010, <http://www.debaird.net/blendededunet/2010/01/study-facebook-and-myspace-enhance-the-positive-relationships-kids-already-have.html> (March 25, 2011).

10. Bill Tancer, "MySpace v. Facebook: Competing Addictions," *Time,* October 24, 2007, <http://www.time.com/time/printout/0,8816,1675244,00.html> (January 29, 2008).

11. Jeremiah Owyang, "A Collection of Social Network Stats for 2010," *Web Strategy*, January 19, 2010, <http://www.web-strategist.com/blog/2010/01/19/a-collection-of-social-network-stats- for-2010/> (March 25, 2011).

12. Michael Arrington, "Facebook Now Nearly Twice the Size of MySpace Worldwide," *TechCrunch*, January 22, 2009, <http://techcrunch.com/2009/01/22/facebook-now-nearly-twice-the-size-of-myspace-worldwide/> (March 25, 2011).

13. Roy Wells, "41.6% of the U.S. Population Has a Facebook Account," *Social Media Today*, August 8, 2010, <http://socialmediatoday.com/index.php?q=roywells1/158020/416-us-population-has-facebook-account> (March 25, 2011).

14. Tancer.

15. Matthew Robson, "How Teenagers Consume Media," *Morgan Stanley*, July 10, 2009, <http://www.debaird.net/blendededunet/2009/07/morgan-stanley-report-on-youth-media-consumption.html> (March 25, 2011).

16. Larry Magid, "Fun and Games," *Staysafe.org for Teenagers*, n.d., <http://www.staysafe.org/teens/protect_yourself/be_smart_online/fun_and_games.html> (January 29, 2008).

17. Ibid.

18. Lenhart, Madden, and Hitlin.

19. Will Lester, "Poll: IM-ing Divides Teens, Adults," *USA Today*, December 8, 2006, <http://www.usatoday.com/tech/news/2006-12-08-im-gap_x.htm?csp=34> (January 29, 2008).

20. Ibid.

21. Amanda Lenhart, Kristen Purcell, Aaron Smith, and Kathryn Zickuhr, "Social Media and Young Adults," *Pew Internet & American Life Project*, February 3, 2010, <http://www.pewinternet.org/Reports/2010/Social-Media-and-Young-Adults/Part-2.aspx?view=all> (March 25, 2011).

22. Erik Sass, "Radio Losing Key Demos: Teens Prefer Personal Devices, College Grads Listen Less," *Media Daily News*, June 9, 2008, <http://www.mediapost.com/publications/index.cfm?fuseaction=Articles.san&s=84209&Nid=43612&p=245679> (March 25, 2011).

Chapter 2. The Family Interface

1. Author's interview with Nancy Willard, May 2008.

2. Amanda Lenhart, Mary Madden, and Paul Hitlin, "Teens and Technology: Youth Are Leading the Transition to a Fully Wired and Mobile Nation," *Pew Internet & American Life Project,* June 27, 2005, <http://www.pewinternet.org> (October 20, 2007).

3. Author's interview with Nancy Willard, May 2008.

4. Ibid.

5. Ibid.

6. "Txt2Connect With Teens: A Parent's TXT Tutorial," *AT&T,* n.d., <http://www.wireless.att.com/learn/messaging-internet/messaging/using-text-messaging.jsp> (May 4, 2011).

7. Claudia Wallis, "The Multitasking Generation," *Time,* March 19, 2006, <http://www.time.com/time/printout/0,8816,1174696,00.html#> (January 29, 2008).

8. Ibid.

9. Ibid.

10. Burt Helm, "Cell Phones Big Brother Would Love," *Business Week Online,* June 15, 2006, <http://www.businessweek.com/technology/contect/jun2006/tc20060614_298933.htm> (January 24, 2008).

11. Ibid.

12. Mark Glaser, "Finding Balance in Teen Use of Social Media," *MediaShift,* October 20, 2006, <http://www.pbs.org/media-shift/2006/10/media_usagefinding_balance_in.html> (January 29, 2008).

Chapter 3. Totally Connected!

1. Author's interview with Nancy Willard, May 2008.

2. Author's interview with Janet Young, March 2008.

3. Stephanie Dunnewind, "R U Still Up? Teens Are Text-messaging Friends Into the Wee Hours," *Seattle Times,* March 31, 2007, <http://community.seattletimes.nwsource.com/archive/?date=20070331&slug=textsleep31> (January 29, 2008).

4. "Phones, Text Messaging and Computers – Teen Sleep Thieves," *About.com,* August 17, 2007, <http://sleepdisorders.about.com/b/2007/08/17/phones-text-messaging-and-computers-teen-sleep-theives.htm> (January 29, 2008).

5. "Sleep Deprivation and Your Health," *About.com,* November 23, 2003, <http://sleepdisorders.about.com/cs/sleepdeprivation/a/depandhealth.htm> (January 29, 2008).

6. "Sleep and Teens," *National Sleep Foundation,* n.d., <http://www.sleepfoundation.org/site/c.huIXKjM0IxF/b.2419127/k.9C6C/Sleep_and_Teens.htm> (May 2008).

7. "Common Sleep Problems," *KidsHealth,* n.d., <http://kidshealth.org/teen/your_body/take_care/sleep.html> (May 31, 2011).

8. Author's interview with Nancy Willard, May 2008.

9. Ibid.

10. Ibid.

11. David Betancourt, "Staying in Touch Only a Thumb Tap Away," *Washington Post,* May 17, 2007, <http://www.washingtonpost.com/wp-dyn/content/article/2007/05/16/AR2007051600649.html> (January 29, 2008).

12. Ibid.

13. Ibid.

14. Alan Fram and Trevor Tompson, "OMG! Teens Use IM 2 Avoid Confrontation," *MSNBC.com,* November 15, 2007, <http://www.msnbc.msn.com/id/21822892/print/1/displaymode/1098/> (January 29, 2008).

15. "When It Comes to Your Life and the Internet, Do You Think You Know It All?" *Web Wise Kids,* n.d., <http://wired.webwisekids.org/index.asp?page=webSafetyQuiz> (May 31, 2011).

16. Yuki Noguchi and Kim Hart, "Teens Find a Ring-Tone in a High-Pitched Repellant," *Washington Post,* June 14, 2006, <http://www.washingtonpost.com/wp-dyn/content/article/2006/06/13/AR2006061301557.html> (May 31, 2011).

17. Daniel Schorn, "Cell Phones: Evolution or Revolution?" *CBS News,* June 13, 2006, <http://www.cbsnews.com/stories/2006/06/08/gentech/main1695676.shtml> (January 29, 2008).

18. Bootie Cosgrove-Mather, "Study: iPods, MP3s Damage Teen Ears," *CBS News,* March 14, 2006, <http://www.cbsnews.com/stories/2006/03/14/health/main1403418.shtml> (January 29, 2008).

Chapter 4. Rebooting School

1. Author's interview with Mark Hershier, May 2008.

2. Author's interview with Diane Conley, May 2008.

3. Ibid.

4. "Critical Issue: Using Technology to Improve Student Achievement," *North Carolina Regional Educational Laboratory,* 2005, <http://www.ncrel.org/sdrs/areas/issues/methods/technlgy/te800.htm> (January 29, 2008).

5. Julie Ray, "System Failure? Teens Rate School Technology," *Gallup Poll,* July 29, 2003, <http://www.gallup.com/poll/8923/System-Failure-Teens-Rate-School-Technology.aspx> (May 31, 2011).

6. Amanda O'Connor, "Instant Messaging: Friend or Foe of Student Writing?" *New Horizons for Learning,* March 2005, <http://www.newhorizons.org/strategies/literacy/oconnor.htm> (January 29, 2008).

7. Jennifer Lee, "I Think, Therefore IM," *New York Times,* September 19, 2002, <http://query.nytimes.com/gst/fullpage.html?res=9F06E5D71230F93AA2575AC0A9649C8B63&sec=&spon=&pagewanted=all> (May 31, 2011).

8. Rosalind S. Helderman, "Click by Click, Teens Polish Writing," *Washington Post,* May 20, 2003, p. B01.

9. Steve Friess, "Yo, Can U Plz Help Me Write English," *USA Today,* March 31, 2003, <http://www.usatoday.com/life/2003-03-31-chat_x.htm> (January 29, 2008).

10. Melissa P. McNamara, "Teens Are Wired . . . And, Yes, It's OK," *CBS News,* June 13, 2006, <http://www.cbsnews.com/stories/2006/06/09/gentech/main1698246.shtml> (October 20, 2007).

11. Leah Hope, "Authorities Make String of Underage Drinking Arrests From Facebook Photos," *ABC Local,* January 14, 2008, <http://abclocal.go.com/wls/story?section=news/local&id=5890815> (January 29, 2008).

12. Isabel Mascarenas, "Tougher Cell Phone Penalties in Schools?" *Tampa Bay's 10 News,* May 18, 2008, <http://www.tampabays10.com/news/local/story.aspx?storyid=80545> (May 31, 2008).

13. "Schools Banning iPods to Beat Cheaters," *USA Today,* April 28, 2007, <http://www.usatoday.com/tech/news/2007-04-27-ipod-cheating_N.htm> (January 29, 2008).

14. "Poll: 1 in 5 Teens Use Web to Cheat," *CBS News,* June 13, 2006, <http://www.cbsnews.com/stories/2006/06/12/gentech/main1701357.shtml> (January 29, 2008).

15. Sherry Saavedra, "Teachers on the Lookout for Teens With Tunes," *SignOnSanDiego.com,* January 8, 2006, <http://www.signonsandiego.com/news/education/20060108-9999-1n8ipods.html> (January 29, 2008).

16. "Schools Banning iPods to Beat Cheaters."

Chapter 5. Exploring Technology's Risks

1. Author's interview with Sarah Swisher, April 2008.

2. "Text Messaging Endangers Teen Drivers," *Edgar Snyder & Associates,* May 2007, <http://www.edgarsnyder.com/news/auto-accident/texting.html> (January 29, 2008).

3. Sarah H. Lynch, "Q&A: Taylor Leming, Texting Motorist," *Time,* June 26, 2008, <http://www.time.com/time/magazine/article/0,9171,1818190,00.html> (March 30, 2011).

4. "Bills, Laws Target Teen Drivers' Cell Phones and Text Messages," *NewsOne6.com,* September 9, 2007, <http://www.newson6.com/story/7729018/bills-laws-target-teen-drivers-cell-phones-and-text-messages> (May 4, 2011).

5. Tim Martin, "Will Bans on Cell Phone Use in Cars Catch Fire?" *MSNBC.com,* May 19, 2008, <http://www.msnbc.msn.com/id/24711916/print/1/displaymode/1098/> (May 26, 2008).

6. "Guide to Cell Phones and Driving," *AAA Washington and Northern Idaho,* n.d., <http://www.aaawa.com/news_safety/traffic_safety/cell_phones.asp> (May 31, 2008).

7. Larry O'Dell, "House Passes Teen Driver Cell Phone Ban," *WTOP News,* February 22, 2007, <http://www.wtopnews.com/index.php?nid=25&sid=1068447> (January 29, 2008).

8. Jennifer Anderson, "California Governor Bans Teens From Cell Phone Use While Driving," *Ergonomics Today,* September 17, 2007, <http://www.ergoweb.com/news/detail.cfm?id=2155> (January 29, 2008).

9. Ibid.

10. "Guide to Cell Phones and Driving,"

11. "Online Games: Game vs. Addiction," *Norton Symantec,* April 25, 2007, <http://www.symantec.com/norton/library/familyresource/article.jsp?aid=fr_onlinegaming_addiction> (January 29, 2008).

12. John Suler, "The Online Disinhibition Effect," *CyberPsychology and Behavior,* vol. 7, November 3, 2004, pp. 321–326.

13. Ibid.

14. Ibid.

15. Ibid.

16. Melissa P. McNamara, "Teens Are Wired . . . And, Yes, It's OK," *CBS News,* June 13, 2006, <http://www.cbsnews.com/stories/2006/06/09/gentech/main1698246.shtml> (May 4, 2011).

17. Ibid.

18. "Text Messaging Privacy," *Yahoo! News,* February 5, 2008, <http://tech.yahoo.com/blogs/hughes/22629/text-messaging-privacy> (May 31, 2008).

19. "When It Comes to Your Life and the Internet, Do You Think You Know It All?" *Web Wise Kids,* n.d., <http://www.webwisekids.org/index.asp?page=webSafetyQuiz> (May 2008).

20. Claudia Wallis, "The Multitasking Generation," *Time,* March 19, 2006, <http://www.time.com/time/printout/0,8816,1174696,00.html#> (January 29, 2008).

21. Ibid.

22. Ellen Lee, "Teens Becoming Savvy About Social Web Sites," *Deseret News,* April 20, 2007, <http://www.deseretnews.com/article/660213422/Teens-becoming-savvy-about-social-Web-sites.html> (May 4, 2011).

23. "Teens, Technology and Drugs: An Inside Look," *MedicineNet.com,* July 19, 2006, <http://www.medicinenet.com/script/main/art.asp?li=MNI%0D%0A&articlekey=62992> (January 29, 2008).

24. Ibid.

25. "Teens & Technology Fact Sheet," *MedicineNet.com,* n.d., <http://www.medicinenet.com/script/main/art.asp?articlekey=62993> (October 20, 2007).

26. "Benefits of Online Interaction for Teens Outweigh Danger, Professor Says," *Science Daily,* November 8, 2007, <http://www.sciencedaily.com/releases/2007/11/071106133103.htm> (January 29, 2008).

27. Ibid.

Chapter 6. Technology Revolution

1. Greg Muller, "By 2012 Today's Teens Will Rule," *The Age,* June 13, 2007, <http://www.theage.com.au/news/business/by-2012-todays-teens-will-rule/2007/06/12/1181414299813.html#> (May 31, 2008).

2. Jonathan Silverstein, "College Campuses Get Social: Social Networking Services on Cell Phones Keep Students and Faculty Connected," *ABC News,* September 11, 2006, <http://abcnews.go.com/Technology/story?id=2411960&page=1> (May 31, 2008).

3. Lauran Neergaard, "Text Messages Could Help Kids Remember Meds," *Mormon Times,* May 13, 2008, <http://www.mormontimes.com/article/12397/Text-messages-could-help-kids-remember-meds> (May 4, 2011).

4. Author's interview with Nancy Willard, May 2006.

5. "Study Finds Teens Increasingly Receiving Advertisements Via Cell Phones," *Newscenter, Ball State University,* February 14, 2005, <http://www.bsu.edu/news/article/0,1370,723-850-30271,00.html> (January 29, 2008).

6. Coco Masters, et al., "A to Z Health Guide 2007: The Year in Medicine," *Time,* December 3, 2007, <http://www.time.com/time/specials/2007/article/0,28804,1685055_1685071_1686158,00.html> (March 30, 2011).

7. Licia Slimon, "It's IM Time: A Case Study of Instant Messaging Reference for Teens at Carnegie Library of Pittsburgh," *Library Student Journal,* September 2006, <http://www.librarystudentjournal.org/index.php/lsj/article/view/35/38> (May 4, 2011).

8. Author's interview with Nancy Willard, May 2006.

9. "The Best Inventions of 2007," *Time,* November 12, 2007, <http://www.time.com/time/specials/2007/0,28757,1677329,00.html> (March 30, 2011).

10. Muller.

Further Reading

Books

Bruce, Linda, Sam Bruce, and Jack Bruce.
Entertainment Technology. Mankato, Minn.:
Smart Apple Media, 2006.

Connolly, Sean. *The Internet and the World Wide Web*.
Mankato, Minn.: Smart Apple Media, 2010.

Jackson, Cari. *Revolution in Computers*. New York:
Marshall Cavendish Benchmark, 2010.

Koellhoffer, Tara, ed. *Computers and Technology*.
New York: Chelsea Clubhouse, 2006.

Schwartz, Heather. *Yourspace: Questioning New
Media*. Mankato, Minn.: Capstone Press, 2009

Internet Addresses

Teens and Technology: Pew Internet & American
Life Project
<http://www.pewinternet.org/Reports/2005/
Teens-and-Technology.aspx>

Teen Tech Buzz Podcast
<http://www.podfeed.net/podcast/
The+Teen+Tech+Buzz/3497>

Web Wise Kids
<http://www.webwisekids.org>

Glossary

aging ear—Loss of the ability to hear high-frequency sounds as ears mature.

benign disinhibition—A phenonmenon in which people share personal things about themselves online that they might not say face-to-face, such as a secret or a fear. This type of sharing can be a lot like "working through" something.

buddy list—A list of screen names of the conversation partners a person typically talks with using instant messaging.

GPS (global positioning system)—A service that can be added to a cell phone or other device to allow another person to tell where the person is by tracking the cell phone or the device.

instant message (IM)—A service that allows users to have real-time conversations with friends. These conversations take place in windows that pop up on the computer screen.

MP3 (MPEG Audio Layer 3)—A type of compressed audio file. These files can be transferred to a portable listening device known as an MP3 player.

mosquito—A high-frequency tone originally designed for shop owners to keep teens from loitering in front of their stores. It has become a popular ring tone for teens hoping to evade adults.

multiplayer game—A type of online game that features role-playing, endless levels of achievement, and an IM/chat function. These games are the most addictive type of online game.

multitasking—The process of splitting time between two or three things at once, such as doing homework, listening to an iPod, and instant messaging friends.

noise-induced hearing loss—Loss caused by listening to something that is too loud for too long (such as an MP3 player). It includes symptoms like inability to hear and ringing in the ears.

online disinhibition effect—A phenomenon in which people say and do things online that they would not do in real life or face-to-face with another person (see also benign disinhibition and toxic disinhibition).

T9 (text on 9 keys)—A type of predictive text that makes texting easier and quicker.

text messaging (texting)—A short-message service found on cell phones that is no longer than 160 characters.

toxic disinhibition—A phenomenon in which people say and do harmful things online that they would not do in person, characterized by rude language, critical remarks, anger, hatred, or threats. It also involves visiting the underworld of the Internet (such as pornography and violent sites). This type of behavior is a type of acting out, and unlike benign disinhibition, it does not lead to personal growth.

Index